PRIVACY MATTERS

PRIVACY MATTERS

Conversations about Surveillance within and beyond the Classroom

EDITED BY
ESTEE BECK
AND LES HUTCHINSON CAMPOS

UNIVERSITY PRESS OF COLORADO
Louisville

Published by Utah State University Press
An imprint of University Press of Colorado
245 Century Circle, Suite 202
Louisville, Colorado 80027

 ASSOCIATION of UNIVERSITY PRESSES   The University Press of Colorado is a proud member of the Association of University Presses.

The University Press of Colorado is a cooperative publishing enterprise sup-
ported, in part, by Adams State University, Colorado State University, Fort
Lewis College, Metropolitan State University of Denver, Regis University,
University of Colorado, University of Northern Colorado, University of
Wyoming, Utah State University, and Western Colorado University.

∞ This paper meets the requirements of the ANSI/NISO Z39.48–1992
(Permanence of Paper).

ISBN: 978-1-64642-030-8 (paperback)
ISBN: 978-1-64642-031-5 (ebook)
https://doi.org/10.7330/9781646420315
Library of Congress Cataloging-in-Publication Data

Names: Beck, Estee, editor. | Campos, Les Hutchinson, editor.
Title: Privacy matters : conversations about surveillance within and beyond the
    classroom / edited by Estee Beck and Les Hutchinson Campos.
Description: Louisville : University Press of Colorado, [2021] | Includes biblio-
    graphical references and index.
Identifiers: LCCN 2020051203 (print) | LCCN 2020051204 (ebook) | ISBN
    9781646420308 (paperback) | ISBN 9781646420315 (ebook)
Subjects: LCSH: English language—Rhetoric—Study and teaching (Higher) |
    Privacy, Right of. | Electronic surveillance.
Classification: LCC PE1404 .P656 2021 (print) | LCC PE1404 (ebook) | DDC
    808/.0420711—dc23
LC record available at https://lccn.loc.gov/2020051203
LC ebook record available at https://lccn.loc.gov/2020051204

Cover photograph, "designated glass 07," © Jef Harris

CONTENTS

ACKNOWLEDGMENTS

All books are collaborative, and many individuals contributed to the development of this collection. Foremost, we thank acquisitions editor Rachael Levay for her belief in this project and for stewarding the compilation through the press. Rachael was our biggest cheerleader, and we are forever indebted to not only her support but also her enthusiasm in helping us get this text to the place it is now. We also thank Dan Pratt, Dan Miller, and Laura Furney for their editorial work on the manuscript, Darrin Pratt for his directorship of the publisher's editorial team, Beth Svinarich for marketing the book, and Kami Day for editing the manuscript. We thank photographer Jef Harris for his generosity with granting permission to use the image of model Anne Mulligan for the front cover for this collection under a CC BY-SA 2.0 license. The editors also offer gratitude to the anonymous peer reviewers for their generous advice, time, and dedication to shaping this collection for the better. These reviewers deserve praise for their insightful feedback, without which this collection would not exist. We extend our gratitude to the contributors of this collection for their labor over the several years of writing and revising up to publication. It was a truly great pleasure to work with every author in these pages. They have reminded us over and over again what it means to *do* scholarship in our discipline. Last, we would like to thank Dànielle Nicole DeVoss for her considerable and generous labor in reading this collection in full and offering her insight into the scholarly contributions this collection presents. She has been a guide and mentor throughout the entire process.

It is with tremendous gratitude that I (Estee) thank my collaborator, coeditor, colleague, and friend Les. During the process of completing this project together, Les's compassionate energy and professionalism pushed this collection forward in positive and fruitful directions. This edited book would not exist if not for Les's brilliance and kindness. In addition, Les is one of the most supportive colleagues I know; she has a rich intellectual history and set of experiences that inform her teaching and scholarship—which makes each interaction and conversation with her a true delight and treasure. I am honored to have worked so closely with her during this project.

I (Estee) also offer my gratitude to current and former colleagues in the Department of English at The University of Texas at Arlington for their encouragement, support, and friendship during the completion of this collection. Foremost, I thank my cohort colleagues Kenton Rambsy and Erin Murrah-Mandril for camaraderie and personal and professional support over the years. For many conversations about productivity with scholarship, I thank Stacy Alaimo. For departmental mentorship with tips for navigating university life, I thank Kevin Porter. I also thank Amy Bernhard, Mike Brittain, Shelley Christie, Cathy Corder, Jackie Fay, Luanne Frank, Kevin Gustafson, Desirée Henderson, Penny Ingram, Margie Jackymack, Joanna Johnson, Laura Kopchick, Peggy Kulesz, Justin Lerberg, Gyde Martin, Neill Matheson, Cedrick May, Tim Morris, Dianne Pearman, Tim Richardson, Ken Roemer, Yael Sasley, Bethan Shaffer, Amy Tigner, Jim Warren, Kathryn Warren, and Chris Worlow for invitations to talk about my work, words of encouragement, and making a positive work environment.

Others have made working on this collection possible through supporting and encouraging me to take a scholarly path toward researching surveillance and privacy concerns within rhetoric and composition, either through conversation or invited talks. I (Estee) thank Megan Adams, Timothy Amidon, Nick Baca, Matthew Bridgewater, Kris Blair, Chris Friend, Jeff Kirchoff, Mariana Grohowski, Gail Hawisher, Lee Nickoson, Joseph Robertshaw, Cindy Selfe, Christine Tulley, and Sue Carter Wood. Finally, I thank Betty and John Thompson, Renée and Eddie Miller, Tonya Thompson, and Trevor and Phillip Gates-Crandall. And for the many hours of patience, care, and housework while I coedited this project, I thank Jared Bingham.

This is the first book I, Les, have published in my life and I owe every single person we've listed above for their considerable labor and love to see this collection to publication and readership. I especially want to thank my coeditor and dear friend, Estee, for her mentorship. This book came together because of your friendship and mentorship. You've gotten me through some of the most challenging moments of graduate school by listening with a compassionate, open heart. Estee, you are brilliant. You are a true leader as you guide by modeling humility, generosity, and curiosity. I'm the scholar I am because you saw me as one since the day we met. Collaborating with you on this collection has taught me much more than editorial work. I know how to be a colleague because of you.

Les also sends her sincerest thanks to her mentors and colleagues who offered her support in the coediting of this collection during her PhD program. She wants to especially thank her dissertation committee for all their support: Dànielle DeVoss, Malea Powell, Stuart Blythe, and Julie Lindquist. Les thanks the following colleagues for their friendship, solidarity, and community: Christina Cedillo, for everything; Maria Novotny, for, too, modeling how to be a generous scholar; Everardo Cuevas, for teaching me how to practice community; Gavin P Johnson, for learning alongside me. This list is inconclusive, but Les thanks (in no particular order) Jaquetta Shade, Catheryn Jennings, Phil Bratta, Bree Matheson, Wilfredo Flores, Thomas Diaz, Estrella Torrez, Dylan AT Miner, the MICCA and IYEP fam, the Indigenous families and ancestors who gave me space to learn more about my Indigeneity in Nkwejong. Lastly, Les would also like to give her deepest thanks to her children, Dan and Zia, for their patience while she worked at all hours to complete her share of this manuscript. Mom loves you both.

PRIVACY MATTERS

INTRODUCTION

Estee Beck and Les Hutchinson Campos

When former private contractor Edward Snowden shared classified CIA documents with *Guardian* reporters in 2013, he emphasized the need for people—and particularly Americans—to know the depths of the surveillance state. The revelations that followed in a series of articles written by Glenn Greenwald set the stage for global outrage and passionate debates about the need for sweeping surveillance systems to protect the sovereign security of the nation from foreign and domestic threats. As years pass and the debates about surveillance rage on, scholars, journalists, legal analysts, social commentators, and the general public argue myriad positions on the efficacy and need for robust surveillance systems. The Pew Research Center reveals that 52 percent of Americans are concerned about their privacy, with the rest in the study ambivalent about what data the government and private corporations collect (2016). While fields such as surveillance studies, communications and media studies, computer science, history, legal studies, and journalism have engaged in conversations about surveillance and privacy, these topics have yet to become part of mainstream scholarship in writing studies. Of the scholarship available in our discipline, most is produced by computers and writing scholars taking a stand against widespread surveillance and the decrease of privacy protections online.

For the past twenty years, teachers and scholars of computers and writing have addressed issues of surveillance and privacy within writing infrastructures through course-management systems, plagiarism-detection software, and social media use in classrooms. These scholars have attended to the decisions teachers face when using digital tools with surveillance capabilities (Amidon et al. 2019; Beck, Grohowski, and Blair 2016; Hawisher and Selfe 1991; Janangelo 1991) or implementing

DOI: 10.7330/9781646420315.c000

plagiarism-detection policies that impact students (Purdy 2009; Zwagerman 2008). The discipline has also discussed the potential harm digital researchers face when collecting data online due to tracking technologies (Hawkes 2007) and how surveillance affects writing program administration and assessment with student portfolios (Crow 2013). More recently, scholarly conversations have focused on the effects of algorithmic surveillance upon identity (Beck 2015); investigations into privacy policies of gaming platforms (Vie 2014); the lasting cultural impacts of doxing private individuals' personal information (Hutchinson 2018); the sharing of consumer data with corporations and governments (McKee 2011; Reyman 2013); and critical digital literacy interventions with regard to health data (Hutchinson and Novotny 2018). Currently absent from these publications is a book-length project within writing studies focused on surveillance both inside and beyond the classroom.

Certainly, countless books, articles, social media posts, white papers, and news articles exist that advocate for less surveillance online and promote increased personal privacy protections. Many of these mainstream resources point to the inequities, ethics, and problems with an ever-watchful surveillance state. These texts seek to challenge discursive normalizations that support surveillance infrastructures and place the onus on the individual: "Don't share what you don't want others to know" and "Don't do anything online you wouldn't want your grandmother to see." As editors, we feel writing studies would benefit from contributing to these conversations with a focused and sustained inquiry into how writing can serve as the vehicle for creating, developing, deploying, and sustaining systems of surveillance. A book-length text examining the impact of surveillance and privacy upon writing and writers makes sense at this kairotic moment because rhetoricians know all too well how close watching impacts social behaviors. It is time, we argue, for rhetoricians to use our training to watch the watchers.[1]

It seems there is very little we do these days that does not involve some sort of surveillance capturing movement and monitoring activity online; from grocery shopping, to driving around town, to going to work, to communicating with loved ones through social media or ordering goods and services from online retailers, our everyday actions are constantly stored in the cloud. The absurdity of tracking millions of people's intimate activities and habits speaks to a late-stage-capitalist increase of large monopolistic corporations controlling economic benefit to the detriment of the moral, ethical, and financial well-being of citizens. And while closed-circuit television technology has been around for some time—and most people accept its presence as a security device—the changing technological landscape of the internet has invited advances in data mining and tracking the creator of the web, Tim Berners-Lee, could have never predicted.

In fact, Berners-Lee's (see Sample 2019) recent observations of the changing internet reveal a concern of the data-tracking technologies that watch what every person does online. In an announcement of a new technology called Solid—a platform allowing users to choose how their data is collected, stored, and used—Berners-Lee wrote optimistically of the connected World Wide Web while acknowledging how the web has "evolved into an engine of inequity and division; swayed by powerful forces who use it for their own agendas" (para 1). He understands the alienation people experience due to late-stage capitalism, that is, the growing gulf between those in power controlling and creating resources people consume while having little recourse to advocate for protection and change. His work also reveals his beliefs about privacy: it matters, and individuals should feel free to act autonomously for their own pursuits. Berners-Lee's work reveals that, through collaboration, along with surveillance and privacy education, people can become empowered to remove their data from the tentacles of corporate interests and government oversight.

Similar to Berners-Lee, Edward Snowden sees the internet as a mass-surveillance system (Mack 2016). His words ring prescient when more and more employers, retailers, governments, and large corporations are turning to big data analytics for key insights into consumer behaviors. This push for big data has been growing since the mid-2000s and, according to a McKinsey and Company research insight, promises companies billions of dollars (Manyika et al. 2011). Academia has not kept itself out of this growing business of data collection. As private industry marshals its considerable resources to purchase software and hire teams of data scientists, higher education has increasingly turned to consultants who offer data analytics on both students and faculty. We find it alarming how companies and consultants obtain data—through complex yet often hidden surveillance methods that use computer algorithms (i.e., mathematical equations used for step-by-step procedures) to highlight, segment, and categorize people's activities into data streams. We also find it alarming how universities continue to participate in similar surveillant practices to validate their brands and also continue to partner with education-technology companies, who often have no oversight in how they use student and faculty data.

For these reasons, we present *Privacy Matters: Conversations about Surveillance within and beyond the Classroom*, which builds from Berners-Lee's sense of collaboration, education, and empowerment by sharing a collection of writings from emerging and established scholars in writing studies. Because of the work writing studies scholars have attended to already, which focus on pedagogy and program administration, the conversations in this collection contribute new culturally situated and community-oriented perspectives on data collection. We have found that to offer unique and impactful scholarship on these topics, scholars must continually keep au courant with new research, policies, and technologies, as surveillance and privacy are not issues contained to just one discipline or within the confines of a particular institution. Therefore, several *Privacy Matters* contributors have specifically responded to our call for interdisciplinary work with surveillance and privacy issues because they recognize everyone—across the globe—is impacted and affected by the erosion of privacy, as well as increased government and corporate surveillance.

WHY PRIVACY MATTERS

As legal and privacy scholar Daniel Solove remarks, one of the problems with defining privacy—especially within legal reform—is the utter disharmony in views about the many distinctions of discretion due to varying subject positions and life experiences. Whereas one person might not object to Facebook maintaining technological logs on Messenger to ensure its operation, that same person might object to Facebook giving read-and-edit access to all private messages sent and received on the social media platform to third parties such as Netflix and Spotify for targeted advertising. Unfortunately, this exact thing happened in 2018 (Newton 2018).

Even though individuals hold a range of positions regarding surveillance and data collection, beliefs about surveillance are often dampened by singular, universal views regarding the safeguarding of people and property. These views tend to reflect conservative and protectionist ideologies. For example, some people seem to think "I've got nothing to hide" when presented with arguments promoting a case for stronger privacy protections. Others seem to think data collection, when experienced online, promotes narcissism because websites and apps deliver personalized advertisements and messages seemingly characteristic of a person's habits, beliefs, or values. Many of those with moderate to liberal positions remain aware of the surveillance state and express concern but continue on with their daily lives with few misgivings about the actors and algorithms that harvest their data. Others may make efforts to read privacy policies or terms of conditions/use statements but sometimes participate in surveilled apps and sites because the benefits outweigh the perceived risks (benefits such as family and friend connections, ease of access, and saving time). Realistically, we all, in some fashion, participate in the surveillance state that has been designed for our social and professional "betterment." Each of these positions is a matter connected to privacy and surveillance.

While this collection does not counter each one of these views (some we sometimes hear our well-meaning students and colleagues express), we acknowledge these refrains because conversations about surveillance and privacy are inextricably bound to political beliefs and cultural values. Assuredly, most people do not outwardly have much to hide in that they are not engaging in criminal activities, nor are they behind the plot of a worldwide revolution. Nevertheless, we agree with Snowden's argument for leaking the massive troves of documents he collected while working with the NSA: we all deserve the right to (1) be made aware of our governments' and institutions' surveillance practices and (2) participate in making, democratically, decisions regarding the data-collection practices that include us, whether we know about them or not.

Privacy, in short, is a topic that matters within and outside the classroom because it is a subject that impacts each person's life no matter their location. We offer this collection at a time when having conversations about privacy means contending with the dynamic complexities of living and working with ubiquitous surveillance. Rhetoricians from a variety of disciplines are well positioned to assess the surge of surveillance occurring offline and online each day. As a result, we hope scholars will be inspired by the chapters in this collection and focus their energies toward persuading industry leaders to reconsider the usefulness of massive data collection, as well as encouraging colleagues to question these practices.

We want to emphasize in our role as rhetoric and writing scholars that privacy matters precisely because everyone remains entrenched in a data-brokerage system that largely goes unchallenged or modified without active, collective resistance and protest. Without knowledge of surveillance functions in our everyday lives, we do not have the means to have a say in how this system appropriates our information. This collection serves as the first book in writing studies to openly call our attention to the importance of starting this conversation.

THREE THEMES EMERGE

In the planning of this collection, the two of us contemplated the scholarly conversations in which our participants were engaging and what specific topics of interest within writing studies their essays addressed. What emerged from our thinking encompassed questions about how surveillance and privacy

impact our teaching, material experiences, and cultural practices. We also noticed these wonderfully smart folks thought
outside the walls of academia and looked to their communities. After talking and planning, we organized this book around
three separate themes we confidentially feel serve as sites for
needed inquiry: surveillance and the classroom, surveillance
and the body, and surveillance and culture.

Each chapter highlights the theme of its section and speaks
to a specific call for others to consider a particular issue of surveillance more critically. We see the themes of these sections as
important to scholars within the rhetoric and writing discipline
because we have come to know surveillance's effects on our
personal and professional lives. Surveillance practices within
our classrooms and universities not only matter but impact our
ability to teach and do research. Part 1 takes up some of those
concerns with critical yet accessible commentary. As monitoring and data collection are built into the very digital infrastructures we use every day, the chapters in part 2 speak to how we
may benefit from more active questioning of certain normalized
technologies and how they impact our bodies. And last, part 3
provides commentary about what happens when surveillance
intrudes on our ability to express ourselves both online and
offline based on who we are.

While we see these themes as representative of conversations
uniquely tailored to scholars in writing studies, we recognize
their value within industry, other professional communities, and
the public at large. Discussions about ethics and technology regularly abound on social media. Today, for instance, our Twitter
feeds are full of academics' comments on Safiya U. Noble's book
Algorithms of Oppression—arguments over whether algorithms are
neutral or not (2018). Since neutrality is still a matter of question, our work must continue. And while Google programmers
like James Damore can hold the opinion that women are biologi-
cally inferior or that facial-recognition software cannot account
for dark-skinned faces, our work must continue. The ideologies
behind the creation of our everyday technologies reflect the people who make them. Our lives, as rhetoricians, ask that we speak

to these injustices as we experience them. To that end, we offer this collection as one text in which this work continues. The sections and their corresponding chapters offered here are our way of speaking back to the injustices of our specific experiences with regard to surveillance and privacy.

CHAPTER ORGANIZATION

Section 1—"Surveillance and Classrooms"—takes a survey approach to integrating discussions of surveillance and privacy into undergraduate courses and administration of programs. The chapters in this section describe the concerns students, faculty, and administrators may share when working with technology that surveils or limits privacy. In chapter 1, Colleen Reilly outlines research-based assignments for courses that help students gain knowledge of surveillance in electronic spaces. The assignments in the chapter are based in part on research and tools developed by the Digital Methods Initiative (DMI) and are designed to make digital surveillance visible. The projects help students understand their digital-data trails and find ways to mask or limit how much data they share online. Next, Jenae Cohn, Norah Fahim, and John Peterson examine, in chapter 2, the collaborative potential of using Google Docs while analyzing the underlying power conditions of teacher surveillance of student activity in those spaces to suggest students can become sousveillers or self-surveillers. Rather than dismissing Google Docs use in the classroom because of surveillance concerns, Cohn, Fahim, and Peterson argue for involving students directly in the surveillance state because it is unavoidable, and such an activity helps students become aware of the surveillance apparatus of Google Docs. Last, Gavin P. Johnson continues the conversation in chapter 3 by discussing the impact data collection has within the university. Johnson argues that grades operate as a technology of surveillance intensified by contemporary neoliberal ideologies and digital infrastructures. By examining previous literature on assessment, evaluation, and big data analytics in writing studies research, he questions how students, teachers, and program administrators surveil and are surveilled by the grades assigned in writing courses.

Section 2—"Surveillance and Bodies"—moves from class-room and program-based instruction into discussions about the material effects of frequently used technologies like fitness trackers and smartphone games. While the authors in this section do consider how these technologies may collide with instruction or with institutional initiatives, the purpose of this section is to address the underlying infrastructures that affect the body. Since surveillance and privacy are topics limited to a discipline or to instruction in higher education, we believe educators and researchers bear responsibility for critiquing the systems that we communicate within or, in effect, that write our lives and our bodies through data. In chapter 4, Dustin Edwards describes how a popular fitness application, MyWellness Cloud, used by his local YMCA, functions in a deep ecology of data brokers, business strategies and policies, proprietary algorithms, and material infrastructures. Edwards analyzes privacy policies and spatial infrastructures to attempt an unraveling of the circulatory activity of bodies in motion that produce data. Chapter 5 continues the conversation about fitness trackers and also integrates a discussion of Canvas, the learning-management system, to assess how big-data mining and academic-learning analytics impact students in different ways. Jason Tham and Ann Duin examine how Oral Roberts University required members of its student body to use fitness trackers. The action raised questions of student privacy. The last chapter in this section addresses privacy policies and ethical considerations. In chapter 6, Stephanie Vie and Jennifer Roth Miller consider how surveillance and privacy play out in social media and gaming spaces by examining *Pokémon Go*. Their case study offers compelling evidence for how written textual information from policy statements provides a means for surveillance of gamer activity.

The chapters in section 3—"Surveillance and Culture"—respond to a need for action globally on matters affecting communities and large segments of populations. In chapter 7, Christina Cedillo examines how surveillance re(inscribes) racial vulnerability in online spaces through three high-profile cases in which academics have spoken out against racism on Twitter, leading to a troubling amount of harassment and public censure. Cedillo presents the experiences of Steven Salaita, Saida Grundy, and Daniel Brewster as case studies that reveal the logics of new racism and the consequences of writing and communicating online under a real-life identity. In chapter 8, Santos Ramos analyzes the rise of Immigration and Customs Enforcement (ICE) within the context of mass surveillance to highlight the shifting dynamics of community organizing among migrant communities post-9/11. Ramos's results show how Homeland Security substantiates a racially driven narrative about legality and how a protectionist state oppresses Latinx communities and Latinx cultural practices. As the closing chapter of section 3, Ramos's piece offers ways to reread or examine the themes emerging from the book. Finally, Dànielle Nicole DeVoss closes the collection with thoughts on the significance of surveillance and privacy for writing studies scholarship and offers a number of questions for future research—questions we hope readers will take up as book-length and article-form projects.

We offer this book as our discipline's first summative academic inquiry into the conversations surrounding surveillance and privacy within rhetoric and writing. As established surveillance studies scholar Mark Andrejevic posits in his forward to *Feminist Surveillance Studies*, "There is no neutral record keeping—all forms of data collection have imperatives built in—and the power of the work assembled here lies in disembedding and exposing these imperatives, the interests they serve, and the uses they enable" (2015, xii). The chapters in *Feminist Surveillance Studies* certainly do the powerful work Andrejevic says they do, and it is in this spirit and purpose that we seek to present our collection. The three sections of this book represent critical perspectives on the topics concerning data collection and often address how surveillance practices disproportionately affect people from marginalized racial and ethnic backgrounds. We had hoped to include chapters that consider surveillance's effects on ability, gender, and sexual identity but did not receive submissions focusing on these needed conversations. We look forward to scholars in the future speaking to them, as we know our collection serves as just a beginning of a vast site of research and intellectual inquiry.

With much enthusiasm, we present this collection to you all in the hopes that you find a spark of a question here and continue the work we are both so passionate about. We thank you for reading and engaging with this book.

NOTE

1.   A nod to Simone Browne's Twitter name and in support of her work in sociology.

REFERENCES

Amidon, Timothy R., Les Hutchinson, Tyanna Herrington, and Jessica Reyman. 2019. "Copyright, Content, and Control: Student Authorship across Educational Platforms." *Kairos* 24 (1). http://kairos.technorhetoric.net/24 .1/topoi/amidon-et-al/index.html.

Andrejevic, Mark. 2015. Forward to *Feminist Surveillance Studies*, edited by Rachel E. Dubrofsky and Soshana Amielle Magnet, ix–xiii. Durham, NC: Duke University Press.

Beck, Estee N. 2015. "The Invisible Digital Identity: Assemblages in Digital Networks." *Computers and Composition* 35: 125–140. doi:10.1016/j.compcom .2015.01.005.

Beck, Estee N., Mariana G. Grohowski, and Kristine L. Blair. 2016. "Subverting Virtual Hierarchies: A Cyberfeminist Critique of Course Management Spaces." In *Making Space: Writing Instruction, Infrastructure, and Multiliteracies*, edited by James Purdy and Dànielle Nicole DeVoss. Ann Arbor: University of Michigan Press.

Crow, Angela. 2013. "Managing Datacloud Decisions and 'Big Data': Understanding Privacy Choices in Terms of Surveillant Assemblages." In *Digital Writing Assessment & Evaluation*, edited by Heidi A. McKee and Dànielle Nicole DeVoss. Logan: Utah State University Press/Computers and Composition Digital Press.

Danmore, James. 2017. "Google's Ideological Echo Chamber: How Bias Clouds Our Thinking about Diversity and Inclusion." July 2017. https://firedfor truth.com/.

Hawisher, Gail E., and Cynthia L. Selfe. 1991. "The Rhetoric of Technology and the Electronic Writing Class." *College Composition and Communication* 42 (1): 55–65.

Hawkes, Lory. 2007. "Impact of Invasive Web Technologies on Digital Research." In *Digital Writing Research: Technologies, Methodologies, and Ethical Issues*, 337–51. Cresskill, NJ: Hampton.

Hutchinson, Les. 2018. "Wielding Power and Doxing Data: How Personal Information Regulates and Controls our Online Selves." In *The Routledge Handbook of Digital Writing and Rhetoric*, edited by Jonathan Alexander and Jacqueline Rhodes, 303–316. New York: Routledge.

Hutchinson, Les, and Maria Novotny. 2018. "Teaching a Critical Digital Literacy of Wearables: A Feminist Surveillance as Care Pedagogy." *Computers and Composition* 50: 105–120.

Janangelo, Joseph. 1991. "Technopower and Technoppression: Some Abuses of Power and Control in Computer-Assisted Writing Environments." *Computers and Composition* 9 (1): 47–64.

Mack, Eric. 2016. "Edward Snowden Warns Your Phone May Be Listening 'Everywhere You Go.'" *Forbes*, November 2. https://www.forbes.com/sites/ericmack/2016/11/02/edward-snowden-warned-about-connected-devices-linked-to-huge-internet-outage/#30aef3842a20.

Manyika, James, Michael Chui, Brad Brown, Jacques Bughin, Richard Dobbs, Charles Roxburgh, and Angela Hung Byers. 2011. "Big Data: The Next Frontier for Innovation, Competition, and Productivity." *McKinsey Digital.* https://www.mckinsey.com/business-functions/digital-mckinsey/our-insights/big-data-the-next-frontier-for-innovation.

McKee, Heidi A. 2011. "Policy Matters Now and in the Future: Net Neutrality, Corporate Data Mining, and Government Surveillance." *Computers and Composition* 28 (4): 276–91.

Newton, Casey. 2018. "Facebook Gave Spotify and Netflix Access to Users' Private Messages." The Verge. Last modified December 19, 2018. https://www.theverge.com/2018/12/18/18147616/facebook-user-data-giveaway-nyt-apple-amazon-spotify-netflix.

Noble, Safia U. 2018. *Algorithms of Oppression.* New York: New York University Press.

Pew Research Center. 2016. "The State of Privacy in America." FactTank News in the Numbers. Last modified January 20, 2016. http://www.pewresearch.org/fact-tank/2016/09/21/the-state-of-privacy-in-america/.

Purdy, James. 2009. "Anxiety and the Archive: Understanding Plagiarism Detection Services as Digital Services." *College Composition and Communication* 26: 65–77.

Reyman, Jessica. 2013. "User Data on the Social Web: Authorship, Agency, and Appropriation." *College English* 75 (5): 513–33.

Sample, Ian. 2019. "Tim Berners-Lee Unveils Global Plan to Save the Web." *The Guardian.* Guardian News and Media, November 24, 2019. https://www.theguardian.com/technology/2019/nov/24/tim-berners-lee-unveils-global-plan-to-save-the-internet.

Solove, Daniel J. 2008. *Understanding Privacy.* Cambridge, MA: Harvard University Press.

Vie, Stephanie. 2014. "'You Are How You Play': Privacy Policies and Data Mining in Social Networking Games." In *Computer Games and Technical Communication: Critical Methods and Applications at the Intersection*, 171–87. Burlington, VT: Ashgate.

Zwagerman, Sean. 2008. "The Scarlet P: Plagiarism, Panopticism, and the Rhetoric of Academic Integrity." *College Composition and Communication* 59 (4): 676–710.

PART I

Surveillance and Classrooms

1

CRITICAL DIGITAL LITERACIES AND ONLINE SURVEILLANCE

Colleen A. Reilly

Students regularly begin their research for writing projects online, searching the web to quickly locate immediate answers. The apparent transparency of search results, carefully cultivated by commercial search engines like Google (1999), obscures the manipulation of results by organizations providing online content. Google alters users' search results based on prior search and browsing history; likewise, Facebook tracks users across the web and presents content to them based on their searches, purchases, and other online interactions. Ubiquitous digital surveillance continues despite users' expressions of discomfort when surveyed about the practice (Purcell, Brenner, and Rainie 2012). To aid students grappling with digital surveillance, writing instructors must expand digital literacies to include students' ability to comprehend, trace, and resist how they are tracked. Additionally, students would benefit from learning how to recognize how the information they receive is invisibly shaped by the digital tools they use to answer their research questions.

This chapter outlines research-based assignments for writing courses that promote students' awareness of surveillance present in electronic spaces and help them recognize how it shapes their knowledge-seeking activities. My assignments are based in part on the research and tools developed by the Digital Methods Initiative (DMI). The DMI's founder, Richard Rogers (2013), promotes online groundedness—a research approach for using data mined from digital spaces to study social and cultural phenomena in physical spaces. This approach highlights the impact of online activities, such as surveillance, on

DOI: 10.7330/9781646420315.c001

the offline experiences of individuals and groups. The assignments proposed in this chapter enlist freely available applications to harness the very processes through which users provide information to commercial interests to expose how organizations monetize users' data and alter their online and offline experiences.

The first assignment employs tools including Lightbeam and Ghostery to detect the presence of social plugins, beacons, and widgets on websites; identify the organizations behind them; and, through Lightbeam, visualize the results. A second assignment goes one step further and prompts students to critique Google's personalization of search results. By creating a research browser free of user data and using a small-data version of Martin Feuz, Matthew Fuller, and Felix Stalder's (2011) big-data research, students develop profiles of categories of users in Google and prompt the search engine to return personalized results. Such assignments, which can be tailored for first-year composition courses, as well as upper-division language-arts courses, empower students to use digital tools through a critical lens; increase their skepticism of the information they locate online; and use the available applications to understand, control, and even reduce the degree of surveillance to which they are subjected.

URGENCY FOR CRITICAL DIGITAL LITERACIES

According to advertisers, digital marketing supports access to free content and services online and provides users with improved experiences, thereby performing constructive functions (Digital Advertising Alliance 2018; Estrada-Jiménez et al. 2016). While the funding model of much digital content relies on advertising revenue, users are disadvantaged in this transaction because they are largely unaware of how the advertising is customized for them and how they as users become the product traded by advertisers (Estrada-Jiménez et al. 2016). As a result, users do not understand why they need to protect their personal information from exploitation and malicious uses in digital spaces. As Estee Beck adroitly explains, users in digital environments interact constantly with virtual objects whose agency requires understanding and interrogation: "The objects not only have an existence, but also provide data and persuade other codes and people to act" (2015, 136–37). To cultivate a more effective approach to these largely invisible but consequential interactions between users and virtual objects in digital spaces, Beck recommends developing an object-oriented rhetorical theory that will "better describe the networks of digital surveillance in online spaces as well as the computer algorithms and tracking technologies that collect data about users" (136). Beck's call corresponds with previous scholarship outlining the multiliteracies essential for working in digital spaces. As Stuart Selber asserts, education must empower students to be critical of current structures in electronic environments and avoid "indoctrination into the value systems of the dominant computer culture" (2004, 234). When instructors ask students to learn in this environment, they have a responsibility to help the students simultaneously develop critical literacies that can provide them with the knowledge and tools to protect themselves.

When first informed of the ubiquity of digital surveillance, many students express ambivalence because they believe they have little to hide. As Stephanie Vie and Jennifer Miller argue in chapter 6, users react to surveillance only after breaches cause them to viscerally experience negative impacts. However, as José Estrada-Jiménez et al. highlight, the risk to users from surveillance activities that collect their data is omnipresent because the trade in personal data and information about online activities potentially compromises users' security and opens them to fraud. Estrada-Jiménez et al. detail the instantaneous process that results in users being served advertisements tailored for them when visiting a website. In short, ad exchanges conduct auctions of a user's profile, which includes everything from the user's browsing history to their age and name; the ad exchange fills the open ad space on the site of a content provider with the ad generated by the advertiser(s) who wins the bid and pays for the right to display the ad to the auctioned user profile (2016,

35). User profiles, like trading cards, are marketed to the highest bidder. The auctions, like high-speed stock trades, are completed instantly, "tak[ing] a few tenths of a second" (35).

The exchange and triangulation of potentially sensitive user information by a large number of actors on any specific content site (through processes such as cookie matching) risk users' privacy and expose them to fraudulent action because the information will inevitably leak through lapses in security: "Information about users along with processed metadata are commonly exchanged in an unencrypted form between ad serving entities" (Estrada-Jiménez et al. 2016, 45). Delfina Malandrino and Vittorio Scarano highlight similar security and privacy concerns resulting from the enormous trove of pseudoanonymous user data currently being collected and distributed. Such pseudoanonymous data can be connected to available "personally identifiable information (i.e., email addresses, full name, address, phone number, fax number, credit card number, social security number, etc.)" through sale by first-party sites to third-party sites and through security breaches (2013, 2834). Because behavioral advertising is growing exponentially, users' data will continue to be collected, auctioned, and sold without their knowledge.

The assignments detailed in the next two sections enable students to understand the degree of digital surveillance they experience and use tools currently available to limit data mining and protect their personal information. Additionally, and more important, the assignments help students imagine and compose questions about digital privacy and security. Because the approaches organizations use to collect information about users is constantly in flux and new privacy tools are continually being developed in response, knowing what questions to ask, what techniques to look for, and which affordances to seek may be the most important literacies to attain.

TRACKING THE TRACKERS

Searching for the phrase *tracking the trackers* online returns results reflecting the level of anxiety around the ubiquitous tracking of users in digital spaces. Most famously, Gary Kovacs, currently the CEO of AVG Technologies, raised awareness about the invisible tracking of users online in a TED Talk about a Firefox add-on called Collusion (2012). This add-on visually represents all the trackers following users across the web, most of which originate from sites the user does not visit. While surveys of citizens in the United States consistently reveal that individuals do not trust corporations with their personal information (GfK 2014), the lack of knowledge about the true scope of the surveillance and the actors involved makes it challenging to harness public opinion to affect policy and legislation. In April 2017, the US Congress and President Trump overturned FCC rules proposed during the Obama administration that would have prohibited internet service providers (ISPs) from selling their users' browsing histories and other personal information. Strikingly, an insufficient number of US citizens were motivated to contact their congressional representatives to prevent this intrusion into their online privacy, possibly because they are not sufficiently educated about what is done with their data and how the government could intervene to protect them.

Awareness is the first step in increasing literacy about the scope of internet surveillance. As CEO of Mozilla, parent company of Firefox, Kovacs (2012) shared this view, which prompted him to develop Collusion, the predecessor to Lightbeam. Lightbeam (https://www.mozilla.org/en-US/lightbeam/) is a Firefox add-on that allows users to visualize the sites they visit and the third-party sites they never visit but that nevertheless track them and collect their data. Lightbeam displays an interactive graph of the visited sites and the third-party sites linked to them, provides the URLs for visited and third-party sites, and displays all sites' server locations by country (if available). For example, when I visited the recipe site Crème de la Crumb (http://www .lecremedelacrumb.com), Lightbeam revealed eighteen third-party sites that partner with the recipe site and potentially track visitors. Some of the third-party sites, such as Google-analytics .com, are ubiquitous—disturbingly, Google's power and proficiency at data collection are such that almost all sites rely on

Google analytics. Lightbeam also revealed that Google analytics' site's server is located in the United States, whereas the third-party site identified as zencdn.net was listed by Lightbeam as associated with an unknown server location. Users can also elect to block particular sites but are warned by Lightbeam that doing so may negatively impact their browsing experience by causing some sites to work incorrectly. Lightbeam has some obvious draw-backs: (1) URLs for third-party sites are identified, but no infor-mation is provided about them beyond their server locations, and (2) insufficient information is provided to users about the ramifi-cations of blocking sites and the types of sites that are most inva-sive and worthy of blocking. Using the URLs of the third-party sites, users can conduct their own research about the organiza-tions responsible for them, but in some cases Lightbeam cannot locate the server and the URL leads nowhere, which is the case with zencdn.net, whose URL returns a server error. Some diffi-culties with Lightbeam could result from Mozilla's having appar-ently abandoned support for the project (Rayl 2015), possibly as a result of Kovac's departure from the company.

Despite its limitations, Lightbeam is a useful tool to employ in introductory writing courses because it is easy to install and offers users who know little about internet tracking a dramatic visual representation of the surveillance to which they are sub-jected. A simple assignment for an introductory writing course would be to ask students to install Lightbeam in their Firefox browser and browse the web normally for a specified period of time, noting the number of visited sites versus third-party sites they encounter. Because the data snowballs very quickly within a brief web-surfing session, students only need to monitor the information produced by Lightbeam for a day or two in order to gather sufficient information to demonstrate that tracking online is pervasive, they interact with many more third-party sites than visited sites, and many of the organizations tracking them are unknown to them. Students can then write a brief report about their findings.

To gain an in-depth understanding of tracking and trackers, students in both introductory and upper-level writing classes can use Ghostery. This accessible browser add-on allows students to gain a basic understanding of the types of tracking and data collection taking place online, the organizations conducting that tracking and data collection, and the policies they follow. While Lightbeam only provides tracking sites' URLs and server locations by country in the form of a graph located in a separate window, Ghostery identifies, categorizes, and blocks an ever-growing number of trackers, revealing to users the trackers' names and providing links to Ghostery's profiles of each tracker and to the tracker's website—all within a drop-down on the user's browser. According the Alan Henry, in a September 15, 2017, post to the blog *Lifehacker*, Ghostery did not begin as a neutral organization but as a commercial enterprise that generated revenue from selling data about advertising blocking to advertisers. In 2017, the consumer operations portion of Ghostery was purchased by Cliqz, a German-based firm focused on web-browser privacy technologies. Evidon, Ghostery's enterprise portion, retains access to provide its clients with "aggregated data about trackers that are contributed anonymously and voluntarily by Ghostery users" (Konrad 2017). Alternate options for privacy protection exist, and students should also be directed to tools like Disconnect (https://disconnect.me) for the most comprehensive privacy solution or Privacy Badger (https://www.eff.org/privacybadger) for not-for-profit privacy protection.

Once Ghostery is installed, students can immediately see a list of the trackers that attempt to collect information and browsing data about them when they access any website. For instance, on the first page of the *New York Times* website, Ghostery detected fourteen trackers and blocked ten of them. Nine of the trackers were advertisers powered by third-party sites seeking to display ads or collect marketing information, four were site analytics trackers that log information about visitors to the site on behalf of the content publisher, and one was the social media tracker linked to Facebook. For each tracker, Ghostery reveals whether it was blocked and provides its name, a brief description of what it does, a link to its Ghostery tracker profile, and a link to the URL of its parent organization. Ghostery's tracker profiles can be potentially generative for student learning. Unlike the link to the organization's website provided by Lightbeam, Ghostery's detailed profiles aid students to formulate questions about tracking organizations. Each profile lists the tracker's aliases; mission "in their own words"; URL; industry affiliations; privacy information and a link to their privacy policies; and a privacy contact, corresponding address, and URL. By examining these tracker profiles, students begin to learn how to interrogate trackers and determine when information is missing or being elided. Under privacy information for Google AdWords, for example, Ghostery reveals that pseudonymous information is collected, as well as users' names, addresses, phone numbers, emails, and logins. Furthermore, the length of data retention is listed as undisclosed. This privacy information may prompt students to consider what information should be collected about them and how long that data should be retained. They might also be prompted to examine the laws and regulations surrounding the types of information that can be collected, sold, and retained. Ghostery provides a useful starting point for this inquiry by displaying consistent information about each tracker.

In an introductory writing class, students could be asked to install Ghostery on their browsers and navigate to a specified list of URLs during a defined period of time. The list of URLs could include publishers, such as *Slate* magazine, commercial sites, government agencies, educational institutions, and nonprofit organizations. Beginning with a common list of URLs facilitates class discussion around the types of trackers located on sites published by different sorts of organizations. Such a project would help students move toward what Steve Mann, Jason Nolan, and Barry Wellman call "sousveillance," "enhancing the ability of people to access and collect data about their surveillance and to neutralize surveillance" (2003, 331). Students may be surprised to learn that nonprofit organizations, perhaps perceived as benign actors on the web, also engage in a significant amount of tracking. For example, on Habitat for Humanity's website (https://www.habitat.org/), Ghostery detected eight trackers, including the site analytics tracker Crazy Egg, whose self-description includes the following alarming language: "Crazy Egg is like a pair of x-ray glasses that lets you see exactly what people are doing on your website. Like, showing you where people are clicking . . . and where they aren't. Or how many people scroll down your pages (and where most people stop). Or where those people are coming from to begin with, and who clicks on what the most" (Ghostery 2020). Learning that this tool is tracking their every click and cataloguing the sites from which they navigated to the Habitat site may disturb students; however, they may be even more unsettled to discover that Crazy Egg collects much personally identifiable information (PII), including names, addresses, phone numbers, and IP addresses, and "shares" that data with third parties, according to Ghostery's description of its privacy policy. Instructors could ask students to visit the specified list of sites, collect screen captures of the trackers Ghostery reveals as active on each site, and examine the profiles of a designated number of different trackers to report on the these trackers' missions and privacy policies. Students could then discuss their findings in class and in written reports to their instructors.

INTERROGATING SEARCH

When seeking information online, most users, including students and instructors, turn to search. Google is the most popular search engine, with an estimated "78.48% of the world's market share of search" (Search Engine Watch 2016); therefore, its operations and policies are central to any investigation of search, particularly for educational purposes. As Jessica Reyman observes, "A student can rarely complete a class assignment without conducting a search on Google" (2013, 514). Google has increasingly collected and harnessed user data to customize and personalize search results. As I have discussed elsewhere, starting in 2005, Google began to increase the personalization of search results, and in 2012, it expanded the categories of user data factored into delivering results to include information from Gmail and Google+, as well as users' geographical locations, search histories, personal sharing, and online social connections (Reilly 2016). As Janae Cohn, Norah Fahim, and John Peterson explain in chapter 2, Google also mines the content of Google Docs to inform the creation of users' profiles and monetize that information. Notably, public outrage prompted Google to discontinue the practice of targeting ads to users based on scanning the content of their Gmail (Bergen 2017).

Google typically justifies mining users' data through arguments similar to those of the marketing and advertising firms discussed above, emphasizing that the increased surveillance results in users receiving improved search results and other services, such as relevant maps, autocomplete results, and YouTube videos (Google 2017). While data mining may increase the expediency of search and other services, personalization of results silos users, delivering the results appropriate for the user profile Google has constructed. Sarah Young (2020) makes a similar point, highlighting that the purpose of much surveillance is social sorting, forging identities for the objects of surveillance and using those identities to categorize individuals for the purpose of commercialization. Targeted marketing has been typical practice; however, the idea that such categorization affects the information users receive when conducting research is more controversial, particularly when the resulting polarization can cause individuals to avoid seeing information with which they disagree. Such fragmentation of information could have major social and cultural consequences.

Users seeking information in digital spaces cannot easily detect the personalization of search because they cannot see what results they may have received had they been a different user. The research team of Feuz, Fuller, and Stalder conducted big-data experiments that allowed them to see personalization in action. They selected three philosophers, Immanuel Kant, Friedrich Nietzsche, and Michel Foucault, and used the indices of seven texts written by each philosopher to submit around six thousand search queries per philosopher in Google to create a specific search-history profile representing the philosopher's perspectives and concerns (2011). Through their analyses, Feuz, Fuller, and Stalder discovered that personalized search results appeared fairly early, within the first two thousand to three thousand queries, and that, based on the search-history profiles created for each philosopher, Google results differed when searching for terms unrelated to the submitted queries, such as software, travel, and neuroscience. These results indicate that Google extrapolates from the queries submitted to categorize users, and through these categorized profiles determines, in this example, the sorts of hotels each philosopher would prefer and their attitudes toward neuroscience. While this strategy may lead users to appropriate results, it also omits or downgrades other results based on assumptions about users, providing them with less varied information that continues to narrow over time (2011).

As my students and I learned in 2013, personalization can be observed with small-scale studies. In a senior seminar related to digital research practices, my students worked in teams of three to create search profiles with identified perspectives on topics such as climate change or hydraulic fracturing. Each student in the team submitted approximately one hundred queries designed to train the search engine to recognize a particular user profile; the terms they used to develop the profiles were often gleaned from websites or publications related to that type of user's perspective on the issues. After developing the search profile, each team member submitted a predetermined list of unrelated terms for items like books, cars, or films, as was done in the larger study by Feuz, Fuller, and Stalder. Small-scale studies such as this are aided by the reality that users rarely examine search results beyond the first page, making that a natural cutoff point for cataloguing results; in fact, according to one study, 92 percent of traffic goes to sites listed on the first page of results (Chitika 2013). My students also observed that each user profile received divergent results for neutral, unrelated terms, which illustrated to the students that personalization affects all searches, not simply those related to obviously controversial or partisan topics. Like Feuz, Fuller, and Stalder (2011), the students realized they could increase result personalization if they clicked on at least one result returned from each query. Completing this research provided students with definitive evidence that personalization of search results is happening and may be affecting the answers they receive from web-based research.

Students also need other research skills to complete this sort of study. To develop appropriate search profiles, students can conduct background research about stances on relevant issues, such as climate change or hydraulic fracturing, and generate a list of terms, much like the terms from the indices of the philosophers' texts, that they can submit to the search engine in order to develop a specific user profile. Students can also use Google Trends (https://trends.google.com/trends/) to locate search terms or phrasal queries that could be productive for this sort of research. Google Trends provides an enormous amount of information about search queries broken down over time and by geographical location; queries are also categorized by subject area and genre searched (websites, images, or videos). Relying on Google Trends also raises issues, for as Safiya Noble demonstrates, students need to be aware that no search terms or results are neutral, making the lists of queries provided by Google Trends a useful starting point but one also in need of interrogation (2012).

To craft a reliable search profile even for a smaller study, the students need to use a research browser, one free from data collected about previous users and browsing sessions. A research browser should begin with a newly downloaded browser, which should be configured so all tracking features such as cookies and browsing history are turned off. This clean browser is used for the control search. When used to create a user profile, the tracking and history features are turned on, but a new browser is needed for the development of each user profile. The DMI provides a useful video that demonstrates how to create a Firefox research browser (2015). The Firefox browser must be used because the DMI has created a Firefox extension to facilitate search-related research, as it describes on its website (2017). By experiencing the challenges of creating and maintaining a

clean research browser, students gain an increased apprecia-
tion of how difficult it is to find results not tailored to their presumed identities.

The small-scale approach to examining search discussed
above can inform individual and group writing assignments,
particularly in upper-level courses. Working in groups, students can create multiple user profiles as described above. The
evidence of personalization comes from the difference in the
order and content of all search results but more strikingly from
the differences in results when terms unrelated to charged subjects are submitted. For example, when my students completed
this sort of work, the group who developed pro- and antifrack-
ing profiles then collected different results for each type of
user when looking for cars or films. The data students collect
should be gathered within consistent time frames, catalogued
systematically, and represented effectively through appropriate
visuals. Providing students with time during class to conduct
searches can be helpful because class time remains constant so
students can control for temporal effects to their search results.
Additionally, students can be encouraged to set up spreadsheets
in an application like Excel to catalogue their results. In terms
of visualization, students might use tables to display top results
along with URLs. They can also characterize the results in some
other way, such as categorizing the results and color coding
them based on the classifications of perspective, subject, or
genre. For instance, a student group who focused on hydraulic
fracturing examined the results for a search of the term *frack-
ing* using pro, anti, and neutral profiles, labeling the top fifteen
results provided to each type of user as positive, negative, or
neutral towards hydraulic fracturing. The neutral search profile
received the most varied results, whereas the other profiles were
provided with predictably skewed results. The students presented a table with the top results for each profile color coded
as positive, negative, or neutral.

While personalization based on search history yields disparate
results for individual users, Andrea Ballatore's study emphasizes
that geographical and temporal relativization proves difficult to

thwart even with a research browser (2015). He introduces Tor (https://www.torproject.org/index.html.en), which provides a browser that distributes user queries over a network of machines, thereby obscuring their geographical origins. When conducting studies that investigate search, students can experiment with the use of tools such as Tor and determine how well they work in comparison to research browsers. Multiple students might conduct the same searches at the same time using research browsers and then using Tor, with the goal of achieving the same results in the same order, at least on the first page of results. This tests the ability of each approach to produce neutral results. Using Tor also raises a host of interesting ethical questions essential to consider in the classroom. As Andy Greenberg explains, most people use Tor simply to browse the web anonymously; however, the privacy afforded allows illegal actors to operate sites, such as a rebirth of the notorious Silk Road site, that avoid surveillance by authorities (2017). In 2017, Tor strengthened its privacy and security tools in response to a breach in 2014, possibly by the FBI. Students can consider whether such tools provide useful protections for users or secrecy for criminals and other dangerous individuals.

BEYOND THE CLASSROOM: ENGAGING IN ADVOCACY, FINDING SOLUTIONS, AND CHANGING BEHAVIOR

As Cohn et al. and Vie and Miller all assert in chapters 2 and 6, respectively, avoiding digital spaces where surveillance occurs is neither possible nor desirable. Instead, as the above assignments illustrate, students can increase their awareness of the degree and mechanisms of surveillance in order to make informed choices and develop agency. The assignments detailed here represent attempts to bring together freely available tools and techniques in creative ways and spur instructors to invent approaches that increase their students' literacies in electronic spaces. Helping students to be conscious of the mechanisms and ubiquity of surveillance and data mining through course projects ultimately prepares and potentially motivates them to engage in advocacy, find solutions to protect their privacy through evolving technologies, and alter their online behavior.

At present, the US government's rules regarding privacy protections and regulations governing the use of consumers' data by ISFs, search engines, phone companies, and other commercial and governmental interests are in flux. The assignments discussed above provide students with a basic understanding of the issues central to privacy and surveillance in electronic spaces so they can become informed citizens and advocate for legal reforms that better protect them from monetization and exploitation. Discussions around tracking by search engines and social media make students aware that these practices are widespread but not inevitable. Guidelines like those put in place by the Obama administration's FCC can be enacted. These proposed rules supposedly have buy-in from commercial interests, as a press release from NCTA-the Internet and Television Association (2017) seems to assert. Additionally, governmental agencies, such as the European Commission (2015) have passed consumer data protection reform rules that include giving citizens access to their own data and a "right to be forgotten," which provides a mechanism for consumers to request that personal data be deleted from commercial databases. Likewise, in 2013, California enacted a Do Not Track law that requires websites to disclose how they respond to users' browsers' Do Not Track signals, which most browsers support, and to provide clear information about the sharing of user data with third parties (Goldman 2013). The assignments above help students understand what laws can accomplish and how to advocate for such statutes. Additionally, empowered students can alert their peers to all forms of digital surveillance by educational institutions, corporations, and governments and argue for protections. Without the consciousness they develop through engaging in the research outlined above, students are less prepared to grapple with the parameters of digital surveillance and imagine solutions.

In addition to becoming advocates, through these projects, students become aware of freely available tools in online spaces that can aid them in protecting their privacy and data from surveillance and theft. As these tools are constantly evolving, learning to use particular tools is less important than understanding what sorts of affordances to seek and how to evaluate their efficacy and safety. For example, Finn Brunton and Helen Nissenbaum's text explains how to use obfuscation to safeguard privacy in public spaces, including digital environments, and details numerous tools and techniques individuals can employ to restrict and subvert data-collection processes (2015). They explain how a technology called CacheCloak hides geographical locations of users on mobile devices from location-based services (LBSs) through interweaving multiple users' locations all at once, obscuring any particular user's trajectory. Additionally, in 2006, Daniel Howe, Helen Nissenbaum, and Vincent Toubiana developed a browser add-on called TrackMeNot that obscures users' identities when searching by submitting automatically generated and randomized search queries to search engines based on "seed lists" of terms connected to specific users so the search engine cannot distinguish between the human-initiated queries and the automated queries (Brunton and Nissenbaum 2015, 13–14). While tools like CacheCloak and TrackMeNot are free and accessible, users may not know how and why to seek them without first understanding the types of surveillance taking place and the protective tools that help users accomplish their aims. Such tools must be sought by users—the tools are not presented to them; users must be literate enough to understand these types of tools exist and know how to successfully locate them.

CONCLUSION

The techniques, tools, and corresponding writing assignments described above prepare students to understand the surveillance they experience in digital spaces and learn to expose it, protect themselves, and advocate for user-centered public policies and legal protections. Merely admonishing students and other users in the abstract that they should be concerned with privacy and resist tracking and personalization is often unsuccessful in propelling them to act. Experiencing the ubiquity of surveillance in digital spaces through research endeavors and corresponding visualization of the results makes invisible privacy intrusions visible and raises consciousness, empowering student users to combat them. Instructors have a responsibility to arm students with critical digital literacies that facilitate that empowerment.

The awareness aspects of critical digital literacy, however, should only be the beginning. While students can use freely available tools to bolster their privacy, they cannot completely protect themselves because the corporations seeking to monetize their information and organizations seeking to exploit their data possess a level of technical expertise and resources individual users cannot match. Furthermore, many protective tools and techniques, such as refusing to post revelatory data on Facebook or LinkedIn, impede individuals' abilities to use the applications to increase their online visibility, which, as Dànielle DeVoss discusses in the epilogue to this volume, is perceived as essential to participating in current social and business enterprises.

All individuals in digital spaces face a paradox, the privacy paradox, which refers to the conflict between individuals' expressed concern over privacy and their apparent willingness to surrender that privacy in online spaces in exchange for very little of value. According to Gordon Hull, the privacy paradox distracts from a more significant paradox: "The self-management model of privacy embedded in notice-and-consent pages . . . can be readily shown to underprotect privacy" (2015, 89). Users' comprehension of and access to protective techniques and technologies online are no match for the constantly evolving data-gathering abilities of corporate and institutional actors. The self-management model's market view of privacy provides users with a false sense of agency, pitting users' capacities for self-management against well-funded and technologically sophisticated corporations that seek to exploit them. This model also distracts users from alternate models that view privacy as a human right. Instructors should promote a higher level of critical digital literacy that helps students recognize and interrogate the problematic paradigms promoted by corporate and institutional actors in electronic spaces and advocate for systemic changes that address this inherent power imbalance in our current electronic spaces.

REFERENCES

Ballatore, Andrea. 2015. "Google Chemtrails: A Methodology to Analyze Topic Representation in Search Engine Results." *First Monday* 20 (7). http:// journals.uic.edu/ojs/index.php/fm/article/view/5597/4652.

Beck, Estee, N. 2015. "The Invisible Digital Identity: Assemblages in Digital Networks." *Computers and Composition* 35: 125–40.

Bergen, Mark. 2017. "Google Will Stop Reading Your Emails for Gmail Ads." *Bloomberg*, June 23. Last updated June 23, 2017. https://www.bloomberg.com /news/articles/2017-06-23/google-will-stop-reading-your-emails-for-gmail-ads.

Brunton, Finn, and Helen Nissenbaum. 2015. *Obfuscation: A User's Guide for Privacy and Protest*. Cambridge: MIT Press.

Chitika, Inc. 2013. *The Value of Google Result Positioning*. Chitika. http://info .chitika.com/uploads/4/9/2/1/49215843/chitikainsights-valueofgoogle resultspositioning.pdf.

Digital Advertising Alliance (DAA). 2018. "Resources for Consumers." https:// digitaladvertisingalliance.org/.

Digital Methods Initiative (DMI). 2015. "The Research Browser." YouTube video, 1:34. https://www.youtube.com/watch?v=bj65Xr9GkJM.

Digital Methods Initiative (DMI). 2017. "DMI Tools Firefox Extension." https:// wiki.digitalmethods.net/Dmi/FirefoxToolBar.

Estrada-Jiménez, José, Javier Parra-Arnau, Ana Rodríguez-Hoyos, and Jordi Forné. 2016. "Online Advertising: Analysis of Privacy Threats and Protection Approaches." *Computer Communications* 100: 32–51.

European Commission. 2015. "Agreement on Commission's EU Data Protection Reform Will Boost Digital Single Market." December 15.

Feuz, Martin, Matthew Fuller, and Felix Stalder. 2011. "Personal Web Searching in the Age of Semantic Capitalism: Diagnosing the Mechanisms of Person-alisation." *First Monday* 16 (2). http://firstmonday.org/ojs/index.php/fm /article/view/3344/2766.

GfK. 2014. "New GfK US Survey Reveals Growing Concerns over Data Privacy, Desire for Corporate and Government Action." GfK. https:// www.businesswire.com/news/home/20140414006027/en/New-GfK-Survey -Reveals-Growing-Concerns-Data.

Ghostery. 2020. "About Crazy Egg." https://apps.ghostery.com/en/apps/crazy _egg.

Goldman, Eric. 2013. "How California's New 'Do-Not-Track' Law Will Hurt Consumers." *Forbes*, October 9. https://www.forbes.com/sites/ericgoldman /2013/10/09/how-californias-new-do-not-track-law-will-hurt-consumers/#6 325dbd475e6.

Google. 1999. "Why Use Google?" Internet Archive Wayback Machine. https:// web.archive.org/web/19991012035335/http://google.com/why_use.html.

Google Safety Center. 2017. "Making It Easy to Understand What Data We Collect and Why." https://privacy.google.com/your-data.html.

Greenberg, Andy. 2017. "It's about to Get Even Easier to Hide on the Dark Web." *Wired*, January 28. https://www.wired.com/2017/01/get-even-easier -hide-dark-web/.

Henry, Alan. 2015. "The Best Browser Extensions That Protect Your Privacy." *Lifehacker*, September 31. http://lifehacker.com/the-best-browser-extensions -that-protect-your-privacy-479408034.

Hull, Gordon. 2015. "Successful Failure: What Foucault Can Teach Us about Privacy Self-Management in a World of Facebook and Big Data." *Ethics and Information Technology* 17 (2): 89–101.

Konrad, Thomas. 2017. "Cliqz Buys Ghostery's Consumer Operations." Cliqz, February 15. https://cliqz.com/en/magazine/press-release-cliqz-acquires -ghostery.

Kovacs, Gary. 2012. "Tracking Our Online Trackers." TED video, 6:33. https:// www.ted.com/talks/gary_kovacs_tracking_the_trackers.

Malandrino, Delfina, and Vittorio Scarano. 2013. "Privacy Leakage on the Web: Diffusion and Countermeasures." *Computer Networks* 57 (14): 2833–55.

Mann, Steve, Jason Nolan, and Barry Wellman. 2003. "Sousveillance: Inventing and Using Wearable Computing Devices for Data Collection in Surveillance Environments." *Surveillance & Society* 1 (3): 331–55. http://www.surveillance -and-society.org.

NCTA-Internet and Television Association. 2017. "Protecting Consumer Privacy Online." January 27. https://www.ncta.com/media/media-room/protecting -consumer-privacy-online.

Noble, Safiya U. 2012. "Missed Connections: What Search Engines Say about Women." *Bitch* 54: 37–41. https://safiyaunoble.files.wordpress.com/2012/ 03/54_search_engines.pdf.

Purcell, Kristen, Joanna Brenner, and Lee Rainie. 2012. "Search Engine Use 2012." Pew Research Center. http://www.pewinternet.org/2012/03/09/ search-engine-use-2012/.

Rayl, Heather. 2015. "Lightbeam." ARLIS/NA: Art Libraries Society of North America, June 2015. https://www.arlisna.org/publications/multimedia -technology-reviews/624-lightbeam.

Reilly, Colleen A. 2016. "Coming to Terms: Critical Approaches to Ubiquitous Digital Surveillance." *Kairos: A Journal of Rhetoric, Technology, and Pedagogy* 20 (2). http://kairos.technorhetoric.net/20.2/topoi/beck-et-al/reilly.html.

Reyman, Jessica. 2013. "User Data on the Social Web: Authorship, Agency, and Appropriation." *College English* 75 (5): 513–33.

Rogers, Richard. 2013. *Digital Methods*. Cambridge: MIT Press.

Search Engine Watch. 2016. "What Are the Top 10 Most Popular Search Engines?," August 8. https://searchenginewatch.com/2016/08/08/what -are-the-top-10-most-popular-search-engines/.

Selber, Stuart A. 2004. *Multiliteracies for a Digital Age*. Carbondale: Southern Illinois University Press.

Young, Sarah. 2020. "Your Digital Alter Ego—The Superhero/Villain You (Never) Wanted Transcending Space and Time?" *Computers and Composition* 55: 1–11.

2

TINKER, TEACHER, SHARER, SPY
Negotiating Surveillance in Online Collaborative Writing Spaces

Jenae Cohn, Norah Fahim, and John Peterson

As teachers who want to democratize the classroom and give as much power to students as we can, we struggle to subvert our own authority in meaningful ways. The three of us—two college-level writing teachers and a teacher/technologist—think of ourselves as resourceful academics in the underresourced world of composition studies. We appreciate how online collaborative tools, such as Google Docs, help the work of decentering by creating shared composing spaces between student and instructor. At the same time, we know that writing technology doesn't decenter the classroom on its own and that using these powerful tools invites surveillance into the collaborative space. Such intrusion extends beyond what we enact as teachers; it is endemic to how telecommunications companies design and conduct business (Yates 1989). We must be critical of our own practices and, as Colleen Reilly stresses in chapter 1, aware of the unintended consequences of working with corporate platforms. We engage with Google Docs because it has become one of the most ubiquitous digital tools used across K–12 and higher education, with more than thirty million students using Google education apps (Singer 2017). While it holds great promise as a collaborative classroom tool, we also reflect here on its potential for overreach.

Even under the corporately structured conditions of Google Docs, the platform's user experience allows students to take on positions of authority by becoming both partners in each other's work and self-aware navigators of the embedded hierarchies and

DOI: 10.7330/9781646420315.c002

power structures of digital platforms. While any massively distributed technology can reinforce colonial and/or corporate thinking, developing self-awareness via critical digital literacy gives
students a framework for negotiating the pitfalls of the contemporary digital landscape. We define critical digital literacy here
in line with Stuart Selber's explanation that developing critical
literacy gives students ways they "might be encouraged to recognize and question the politics of computers" (2004, 75). Given
the choices students make in composing within different word-
processing programs, we find it essential to employ Google Docs
in ways that help students understand how their behaviors, practices, and experiences of writing online may be impacted differently than when using other word processors. Exposing these
politics of the interface may not necessarily yield to dismissal
of or reluctance to use the platform entirely. In fact, we argue
that Google Docs makes work in a classroom more transparent;
when we use shared spaces, we invite students to act as agents in
their own learning. We support this argument by drawing attention to Google licensing agreements and situating the ubiquity
of Google Docs among other teaching choices. We illustrate the
potential and challenges of Google Docs by sharing three instructor narratives, including activity descriptions, of teaching collaborative writing within Google Docs. We conclude with a call for
instructors' continued pedagogical action to foster critical, functional, and rhetorical awareness of surveillance technologies.

CONTEXT

In "The Rhetoric of Technology and the Electronic Writing
Class," Gail Hawisher and Cynthia Selfe warn against reproducing power structures through technology. In invoking Michel
Foucault's panopticon, they point to how teachers might "use
networks . . . as disciplinary mechanisms for observing students'
intellectual contributions to written discussions" (1991, 63),
and they observe how such surveillance encourages students to
perform "self-discipline" (63) and conform to social and institutional expectations. Hawisher and Selfe were prescient; they

saw technology helped students learn from each other's work but understood how power relationships had to be addressed as the means for technological surveillance advanced. We see this concern complicated even more as research in online privacy suggests that while people tend to claim they care about their online privacy, they rarely adjust privacy settings to address these concerns (Saeri et al. 2014). The power a large corporation gains by conducting surveillance while offering free services helps construct a system in which users may be unaware of how the structure shapes their behaviors. We believe teachers can help students negotiate this power differential by building awareness of digital surveillance.

CONSUMER DATA AND GOOGLE POLICIES

Since Google Docs structures classroom interaction, we assert instructors must maintain a high degree of cognizance of the politics behind the tools they use. Google has been a market leader, in large part because it profits from surveilling its consumers. Until 2017, this profit model was reserved for private companies, but with the House and Senate 2017 decision to allow internet service providers like Comcast, Verizon, and AT&T to sell their consumers' data for private gain, surveillance became further normalized in US telecommunications (Wheeler, *New York Times*, March 29, 2017). As others in this book point out, examining the political conditions of teaching tools is more important than ever. And, in this chapter we build on from these contributions with the assertions of Stephen Wiley and Mark Root-Wiley (2007): "Technologies are not value-neutral tools or liberatory spaces in which identity can be freely constructed, but manifestations of specific historical arrangements of power, agency, and subjectivity."

Take the case of Google's privacy policy, which assures users that their intellectual property remains their own although the policy informs users that everything else they produce in Google Docs is up for the company's discretionary use. Their 2017 privacy policy sets these conditions:

When you upload, submit, store, send or receive content to or through our Services, you give Google (and those we work with) a worldwide license to use, host, store, reproduce, modify, create derivative works (such as those resulting from translations, adaptations or other changes we make so that your content works better with our Services), communicate, publish, publicly perform, publicly display and distribute such content. (Google 2017)

Google profits from all work produced within its products. It tracks and scans documents for patterns, then sells bundled consumer information to marketers. We found exceptions for college licenses; in a December 2, 2015, blog post titled "The Facts about Student Data Privacy in Google Apps for Education and Chromebooks," Jonathan Rochelle, Google's director of education apps, claimed student data would not be used for developing ads targeting those users. As we understand it, Google can still aggregate data to assess marketing opportunities. One typical example of Google Docs harvesting information is the Explore button in the corner of the document. This feature finds keywords in documents and matches them instantly with search results from across the web; in effect, this selection co-opts key phrases from a writer's work into a massive Google search. Purportedly, this feature is intended to help writers find source material, but the Explore button remains another method for Google to learn about what information interests its users[1]—and how it can continue to refine and privilege search results and advertisements that align with those interests. Thus, we take the position that students and teachers must discuss consequences such as these. Sharing knowledge of how Google Docs features both assist and exploit users allows educators to pursue critical digital literacy.

CONSIDERING GOOGLE DOCS AMONG OTHER COLLABORATIVE TOOLS

Knowing this corporate context structures students' learning, we acknowledge the enormous challenge of using technology that potentially reproduces oppressive power structures. Many could argue students can't be critical of a surveillance state once they're within it because they're not aware of alternatives—just look to Foucault for this acknowledgement. To avoid these problems, we could ask students not to use Google Docs or pursue any activity online at all. However, we believe removing students from contexts where they will likely work and learn would be irresponsible and impractical for educators. Rather than isolate students from these environments, we involve them directly to help them develop an awareness of the politics of their tool use, and in so doing, develop critical digital literacy. Ideally, instructor guidance in navigating surveilled platforms offers an effective countervailing force to obvious dangers of working within powerful digital environments (Beck 2016; O'Byrne 2017). In other words, by avoiding Google Docs, we also avoid an opportunity to consider how a popular tool operates in our current web ecosystem. Does that mean Google Docs is the "best" tool in terms of advancing ethical, or in Audrey Watters's words "convivial," teaching (2014)? No. But its increasing, widespread use by teachers starting as early as elementary school is evidence that the tool is firmly part of education culture. As postsecondary writing teachers, we are positioned to help students adopt sophisticated understandings of this powerful, adaptable, and free tool.

When adopting software due to pragmatic factors like convenience, instructors must help their students develop a critical understanding of data ethics. It also means that we, as authors of this chapter and as teachers, accept the realities of pedagogical practice. For example, while there are many competitors to Google Docs[2]—some not linked to a corporate infrastructure—many teachers can't adopt these platforms because they work within severe resource limitations. Tools such as Eli Review, developed by composition researchers and instructors, offer promising alternatives, but institutional subscription costs and IT maintenance priorities can make such alternatives unfeasible. Even instructors who may have additional resources use Google Docs precisely because it is a tool powered on a reliable server, which operates virtually without service disruption.

Our discussion herein accepts pragmatic conditions as part of the investigation of pedagogical practice. We make this choice while engaging with the risks of this choice.

GOOGLE DOCS AND PEDAGOGY

At the intersection of surveillance studies and writing studies is the question of power and how using digital technologies potentially reproduces institutional hierarchies. When instructors and students build documents together, rather than instructors looking over the shoulders of students when they compose, this space theoretically mediates instructor privilege and reinforces pedagogical practices that share power. For Google Docs, the platform makes the writing process transparent to both students and teachers in its real-time interactivity with multiple participants. The platform also shows all users where and when changes have been made. The ability to update synchronously allows collaboration without disruption or time limitations. Since all users have version control, that is, access to older versions of the document, they can revert back to earlier versions without losing data, and this high degree of flexibility and transparency facilitates lively exchange.

For all the possibilities of power distribution among teacher and students, a problematic side of Google Docs remains. We acknowledge students are not only consumers of information but also producers within corporate-sponsored, networked spaces. If we take Foucault's (1977) view that systems of technological surveillance are a necessity of professional, personal, and civic life, we must support students' development of critical digital literacies within these landscapes.

TEACHING NARRATIVES

As teachers, we invite students to respond to surveillance when we design activities that counter passive use of surveilled platforms. This section offers teaching narratives as examples of how the classroom space is a viable site for engaging students as coinvestigators in pedagogy and perhaps, at times, turning the gaze back on the surveillance culture represented by Google Docs. These narratives, composed in the first-person voice of each author, extend the idea that Google Docs can be used to democratize the writing classroom and simultaneously activate critical digital literacy.

Jenae's Teacher-to-Student Interactions: Creating
a Shared Content Repository

This first example of teacher-to-student interaction in Google Docs illustrates how Jenae uses Google Docs as a way to create a shared class repository about a particular class topic and to facilitate critical digital literacies.

To brainstorm shared knowledge of our course concepts, I invited students into Google Docs so each could work in the same document at the same time while using their own devices. I wanted everyone to see exactly what their peers produced. I hoped this setup would avoid the problem of multiple students sharing similar contributions; by seeing each other's ideas appear synchronously, students could add novel contributions to the group.

I explained we were using Google Docs to create a shared repository of ideas about a course topic. In order to understand what experiences students had with using Google Docs in the past, I then conducted a poll, which showed that nearly all the class members had some prior exposure to the platform. This knowledge was useful to me as the instructor because it allowed me to prune back functional instructions and instead focus on critical engagement with the platform. Before the students dove into the document, I specified that we would look at each other's ideas and build on what we saw. I framed the activity as purposefully inviting "chaos," with everyone working in the same document, in the same room, at the same time, and explained that this chaos was part of the collaborative process. I then divided students into small groups, with each group responsible for filling in a portion of a chart in the shared document. Students formed responses concurrently and modulated their writing to mesh with other contributions. In practicing this decision-making, they heightened their awareness of how writers make choices depending on the rhetorical situation and audience while also recognizing how the platform's constraints and affordances could shape their interactions.

I kept the document open on a screen at the front of the room for all to view. During the activity, I felt hesitant to watch what they were doing, but the process of watching through the document, rather than peering over shoulders, actually felt less invasive; seeing the products of their work, removed from their embodied selves, allowed me to assess the progress of the product they created rather than individual progress. My self-consciousness was an attempt not to fall into the teacher-centric patterns Hawisher and Selfe warn us about (1991). By watching the group work in a projected space on the screen, I saw my role of teacher as one facilitating critical awareness of the digital space. Even though students knew I watched their progress, they could see that what I monitored were not individual efforts but group progress. The surveillance enabled our class community to understand the full conversation's movement rather than any one individual's unique contributions.

In contrast to previous group work, composing in Google Docs changed the dynamic of our discussion; the class became a unified creator of content, and I became a facilitator. By seeing this process happen in real time, students developed some awareness that their writing processes could be dramatically informed by their platform choice and by participating in surveilled group writing. Conversation flourished, and students collaboratively curated the final product before instructor intervention. Through bringing this conversation into the space of Google Docs—instead of a discussion forum, for example—students could see in real time the extent to which the platform shapes the final products of their work, thereby enabling the development of critical digital literacy.

John's Students-Teaching-Students: Building Digital
Literacy through Google-Level Research

John describes a collaborative activity in which students in their first week of class use a Google Docs search feature, Explore, to see how their ideas about a topic fit within the context of a larger digital conversation. By collaborating to contribute to existing research, students learn ways to function within the landscape with a higher degree of digital literacy, to teach each other how they can raise ideas, and to develop greater critical awareness of what finding sources in digital environments entails.

Like many teachers, I ask students to post their responses to readings in Google Docs. In this exercise, students broke into small groups, selected one of their responses, completed some group research, and rewrote the response collaboratively for an audience beyond the class. To define this new audience, students activated the Explore function, which scanned their classmate's file for words and phrases that matched within a Google search. Students could then see how the language they used in responses ideas, phrasing, intertextual references was being used by scholars across the digital landscape. The goals of the activity were simple: learn to rewrite for different audiences; learn what it's like to be in "conversation" with other researchers; and learn to develop critical digital literacy.

The Explore function searches a file for virtually any matches and retrieves dozens of results. I encouraged groups to review results that included topics overlapping with the selected student's response. Since the reading was a memoir about the process of getting into college, one group found short articles about student stress, alcohol use, and standardized testing. The group then decided which topic and which researched article they would use to focus their rewrite. Since they knew they had to choose something about the text's overall topic (getting into college) and the topic of a short article, they chose a piece on standardized testing. Next, they all read the piece (found collaboratively with Explore). The most productive—and challenging—step for the group included figuring out the audience for the revision.

Students negotiated at length about strategies they would use for rewriting. When I urged them to start writing, they assigned each other sentences and talked aloud to explain their decisions. They discussed what information the audience would need to understand the context of their claims. As Jenae saw with her students, since everyone could both write and see what others were writing, they could adjust the "voice" of the piece to match.

In a written reflection, one student noted, "By searching for the article that would fit best within our discussion, I found out that there were many different viewpoints focused around the same points, and it was difficult to find the exact one we were thinking of." This student saw not only that multiple scholars might take multiple pathways to get to the same point but that doing research meant developing the critical awareness to select from and weigh a range of digital sources. By collaborating and using Explore, the students taught each other how intellectual tension was part of doing research. They also learned how to develop their own voices within a digital conversation; they were both researching in a digital landscape and contributing to it, thus going beyond merely borrowing research via Google.

Another function of Explore is a search for matches within the user's own space on Google Drive, the cloud storage Google provides users along with its platforms. I reminded students that Explore was evidence that Google was aggregating their intellectual property and pointed out they were crafting their digital identities every time they worked in Drive. When I asked what they thought of Google surveilling their data, the general reaction was that it was not a problem. One said "Cool." Even as we interrogated the consequences of this acquiescence, student concern remained low; we returned to this question throughout the course. I must confess that, although I was concerned with this neutral reaction, this gave us an opportunity to talk about how digital tools are not value neutral. In a sense, the students' thrill of discovering entry into a digital conversation and worrying about how they achieved this entry were at odds. I understand this tension as an ongoing and productive part of developing critical digital literacy.

A significant complication, of course, is how this activity led students to go to Google first for their research. When one student commented, "I feel like Google is a reliable source," it reflected a common misinterpretation—that Google is a source and that it is reliable. While I trust this student meant it felt good to use a tool that helped research complex concepts, it also was a sign we would need to talk about the difference between a search engine and source and delve into ways to evaluate reliability. This student's misinterpretation presented an opportunity to spotlight the significant limitations of Google. The Explore feature kick-started awareness of the digital landscape, and we next moved into library database searches of journal articles. When students engaged the Explore feature and saw its limitations, they taught each other to develop a research ethos that aspires far beyond Google.

Student-to-Student Interactions: Collaboration within a Surveilled Writing Platform

This example discusses student-to-student interactions in Google Docs. Norah shares her reflections on students' interactions and also instructor reflections that helped guide her pedagogical decisions.

My reasoning for using Google Docs was quite straightforward: I wanted a user-friendly and synchronous platform to provide students with more control over the process of sharing their writing. I had previously worked with the built-in peer-review feature on Canvas, but students had less control over sharing their documents, and they could not see each other's comments appear in real time.

Understandably, some students may find that others' ability to trace all their changes infringes upon their sense of privacy[3] or even heightens their sense of insecurity regarding their decisions as authors. While tracing changes is not obviously an intrusive invasion of privacy, some students do prefer to make revisions in private. Acknowledging a writer's own preferences and feelings is an important part of encouraging critical digital literacy, which involves self-awareness of one's own boundaries and privacy needs. In their heightened sense of the value of individual needs, my students made me aware of (unanticipated) positive interactions within Google Docs. I noted that in several instances, as students conducted peer review in person, they chose to "chat" virtually in their feedback process using Google Docs. I noticed that as one student commented on their peer's paper, the author would reply back through the comment thread. As I saw it, using this platform helped reflect "the reality of the real world where group work is increasingly valued in the workplace and where collaborative writing is a common practice" (Strauss 2001, quoted in Wigglesworth and Storch 2009). Google Docs allowed them to become better and perhaps more familiar collaborators, with a stronger sense of focus on their task.

While students followed guidelines I set up in a worksheet, their comments went beyond responding to required questions and instead became a tool of encouragement, a place to pose reflective questions, and a space to post helpful links and even to offer some humor! Emojis and memes made their way into their peers' original drafts, and in those instances, the peer-review process became much more amicable and organic. One student commented through course evaluations that "Google Docs was useful because it was easy to share, edit, and comment when peer reviewing. Also, working together on a document in real time with others was useful." In such instances, I found this interactive tool allowed students to see that "academic research is a continuous progression of learning, sharing and building upon work of others" (McCollum 2012).

Through numerous class collaborations I realized this online platform could potentially represent a site for a community of practice, a CoP (Lave and Wenger 1991). This mediated online platform also gives students an alternative to in-person interaction. For some students, adding comments and responding helps define the exact issue in a mediated and perhaps safer space before embarking on a face-to-face discussion.

While I was prone to embrace the merits of how such a platform helps democratize composition and revision among collaborators (Evans and Bunting 2012), I knew this mediated space contributes to the type of surveillance Hawisher and Selfe warn writing teachers about in computer-mediated classrooms (1991). Admittedly, I later developed greater hesitation when I became fully aware of the level of surveillance Google Docs provides when I clicked on the See New Changes tab at the top of the page. For assignments in which I asked students to carry out their entire drafting process on Google Docs, I could see how much time each spent editing. I also knew whether revisions happened over a period of days or in one sitting. Moreover, I could access which edits were a direct response to my suggestions and where students chose to forego editing. This level of surveillance gave me pause because it caused me to question whether I developed biases in evaluating their work. I realized I was inclined to believe a student had done "better" revisions if they revised over multiple days rather than all at once. By viewing the back end of different iterations, teachers have an insider's view of a product that has seen the labor of many ideas and versions. I think educators should acknowledge the messiness of the students' writing process and showcase this messiness as examples of productive student writing within a genuinely collaborative and mediated space. Moreover, we must question our biases on what we perceive to be "good" writing practices and provide more opportunities for in-class discussions with our students on what constitutes a good writing process for them as well.

DISCUSSION

Negotiating the concerns with surveillance in our classrooms requires flexibility and awareness of how privacy policies and data usage change alongside technological changes. By helping our students understand the relationship between these policies and our platform usage, we bring critical digital literacy instruction explicitly into our teaching practice. Our instructor narratives are attempts at negotiating both the powers and the risks of Google Docs in our classroom, but our approaches will change as Google Docs shifts its functions within the larger digital ecosystem. Even in our process of composing this chapter, we needed to revise our framing and context around Google's shifting privacy policies and the larger culture of surveillance in the United States (Kang, *New York Times*, March 17, 2017). Users are leaving behind increasingly large digital footprints (Beck 2016), and it is our responsibility as instructors to help students understand what that footprint looks like and what forms it can take. A single Google profile can be integrated across Google tools, from Docs to Maps to Search. We cannot deny that our identities on the web grow increasingly visible as we participate in a digital ecosystem. The degree to which students are concerned about the implications of this participation remains for us an area of study. In this chapter, we argue that Google Docs offers powerful affordances and limitations in teaching, learning, and living in a digitally surveilled environment. Within this landscape we can work within Google Docs to invite a multiplicity of perspectives and to encourage students to see the impacts of access to each other's writing.

Our teacher narratives emphasize the power of students working together on one document in a shared space. Students report deepened investment in collaborative writing because Google Docs makes the fruits of that collaborative labor visible to them. This collaborative work in turn enhances a shared, critical understanding of how digital platforms are both shaping their writing and potentially surveilling their content. If we asked students to write in Google Docs individually, they might not develop an awareness of how digital platforms breach individual privacy. However, by turning the moment of using Google Docs into a collaborative experience, the potential for privacy breach becomes all the more visible as multiple students (and instructors) engage in the space together, uncovering a critical understanding of all of the platform's possibilities. Google Docs is not just yet another word processor; it is a space that exists on a public web. We recognize that even when a shared collaborative space attempts to democratize perspectives in the classroom, we still elide individual differences and may not fully acknowledge how the shared space emerges from school, a place with its own long history of institutional racism, sexism, and elitism. What's more, Google Docs' corporate presence represents a surveillance state we use and critique simultaneously. There is more work we as scholars, pedagogues, and practitioners can do to engage in practices that show how our embodied spaces can promote greater equity. We further acknowledge we need to research student perspectives on this experience in greater depth and see that future research could investigate students' individual perspectives to understand the work of identity renegotiation within collaborative writing spaces.

One of the key components in creating a collaborative space is making technological mediation visible. This visibility has always been important—even before the social web—but becomes more urgent when our technologies may be influenced by inequitable ideologies. The project of adopting equitable practices in our classrooms is a large one and starts with making our technologies and their ideologies visible. Only then can we start radically reshaping the teaching and learning practices that follow.

CONCLUSION

As teachers, it's our job to ask students to engage in an ongoing conversation about the implications of using technology for communication and invite them to negotiate openly within collaborative writing spaces. Indeed, other authors in this book invite readers to reflect on how the metaphor of the panopticon helps us see how students self-regulate and feel compelled to fall in line with institutional and teacher expectations. At the same time, we argue that it is useful to refresh in students this awareness of how any participants in a system can at times internalize the ideologies of authority. Perhaps teachers' most fundamental level of responsibility is to assure that we or our students are not unwittingly reproducing structural inequities.

We may not be able to change the entire landscape of reading, writing, and communicating within a public web. What we can change is our students' awareness of how to operate online so they can be fully cognizant of the implications of their activities. Through teaching collaborative document composing within major proprietary software like Google Docs, we draw student attention back to the interfaces of their writing. In so doing, we support them in becoming more critical consumers of the technologies that may otherwise be invisible to them. When we can make matters of privacy visible again, we give agency back to our students to decide how, when, and with whom they'll use particular platforms for their writing, both within and beyond the university.

NOTES

1. One teaching narrative below describes an activity designed for students to exploit the Explore function and become aware of how it interacts with a user's digital identity.

2. Alternatives include Etherpad (http://etherpad.org/), an Open Source synchronous composing tool; Word Online (https://office.live.com/start /Word.aspx), a tool that offers a free collaborative writing space as long as users have a Microsoft account; and Fidus Writer (https://www.fidus writer.org/), a collaborative composing tool designed primarily with an academic audience in mind.

3. One option is to let students work outside Google Docs for other activities.

REFERENCES

Beck, Estee N. 2016. "Writing Educator Responsibilities for Discussing the History and Practice of Surveillance & Privacy in Writing Classrooms." *Kairos: A Journal of Rhetoric, Technology, and Pedagogy* 20 (2). http://technorhetoric .net/20.2/topoi/beck-et-al/index.html.

Evans, Donna J., and Ben Bunting Jr. 2012. "Cooperative and Collaborative Writing with Google Docs." In *Collaborative Learning and Writing: Essays on Using Small Groups in Teaching English and Composition,* edited by Kathleen M. Hunzer. Jefferson, NC: McFarland & Company, 109–29.

Foucault, Michel. 1977. *Discipline and Punish: The Birth of the Prison.* New York: Random House.

Google. 2017. "Terms of Service." https://policies.google.com/terms?hl=en -US.

Hawisher, Gail, and Cynthia Selfe. 1991. "The Rhetoric of Technology and the Electronic Writing Class." *College Composition and Communication* 42 (1): 55–65.

Lave, Jean, and Etienne Wenger. 1991. *Situated Learning: Legitimate Peripheral Participation.* Cambridge: Cambridge University Press.

McCollum, Robb M. 2012. "Working Together Towards Greatness: The Cumulative Writing Mode and English Language Learners." In *Collaborative Learning and Writing: Essays on Using Small Groups in Teaching English and Composition,* edited by Kathleen M. Hunzer, 201–16. Jefferson, NC: McFarland & Company.

McKee, Heidi A. 2016. "Protecting Net Neutrality and the Infrastructure of Internet Delivery: Considerations for Our Past, Present, and Future." *Kairos: A Journal of Rhetoric, Technology, and Pedagogy* 20 (2). http://kairos.technorhetoric.net/20.2/topoi/beck-et-al/mckee.html.

O'Byrne, Ian. 2017. "Wakefulness and Digitally Engaged Publics." *Hybrid Pedagogy,* April 12. https://hybridpedagogy.org/wakefulness-digitally-engaged-publics/.

Rochelle, Jonathan. 2015. "The Facts about Student Data Privacy in Google Apps for Education and Chromebooks." Google for Education blog. http://googleforeducation.blogspot.com/2015/12/the-facts-about-student-data-privacy-in.html.

Saeri, Alexander K., Claudette Ogilvie, Stephen T. La Macchia, Joanne R. Smith, and Winnifred R. Louis. 2014. "Predicting Facebook Users' Online Privacy Protection: Risk, Trust, Norm Focus Theory, and the Theory of Planned Behavior." *Journal of Social Psychology* 154 (4): 352–69. https://doi.org/10.1080/00224545.2014.914881.

Selber, Stuart. 2004. *Multiliteracies for a Digital Age.* Carbondale: Southern Illinois University Press.

Singer, Natasha. 2017. "How Google Took over the Classroom." *The New York Times,* May 13, 2017. *NYTimes*.com. https://www.nytimes.com/2017/05/13/technology/google-education-chromebooks-schools.html.

Watters, Audrey. 2014. "Convivial Tools in an Age of Surveillance." *Hybrid Pedagogy,* July 5. hybridpedagogy.org/convivial-tools-age-surveillance/.

Wiley, Steve, and Mark Root-Wiley. 2007. "Identification, Please: Communication and Control in an Online Learning Environment." *Kairos: A Journal of Rhetoric, Technology, and Pedagogy* 11 (2). http://kairos.technorhetoric.net/11.2/topoi/wiley/index.html.

Wigglesworth, Gillian, and Neomy Storch. 2009. "Pair Versus Individual Writing: Effects on Fluency, Complexity and Accuracy." *Language Testing* 26 (3): 445–66.

Yates, Joanne. 1989. *Control through Communication: The Rise of System in American Management.* Baltimore: Johns Hopkins University Press.

3

GRADES AS A TECHNOLOGY OF SURVEILLANCE
Normalization, Control, and Big Data in the Teaching of Writing

Gavin P. Johnson

In August 2015, I found myself in a classroom crowded with other graduate students preparing to teach first-year writing. Midway through a week-long teacher-training workshop, one of the writing program administrators provided a sample student paper and announced, "Using the tools we've discussed, read, provide feedback, and grade this paper. Then, in small groups, discuss your grades and see if you can reach consensus. Finally, we'll go around the room and compare." Twenty-five minutes and a few pages filled with scribbles later, I prepared to discuss my grade for this anonymous student paper. "Overall, I thought the ideas were good, and I like the author's style, but I see some issues with organization and research integration." I paused. "So . . . I gave it a B." In my small group, the other soon-to-be teachers offered two As, an A-, and a B. As a group, we discussed our feedback and settled on an A- for the paper. Easy enough. When we went around the room, the other groups offered their negotiated grades: A, A-, B, and C. A range of grades on a single paper from a group of teachers a week away from teaching the same curriculum. The room erupted in panic: "Am I doing something wrong?" "Am I being too harsh?" "I refuse to give up my rigor!" "I know what an A paper looks like!"

As teachers of writing, we inevitably discuss grades and grading practices. No matter what curriculum we follow and what pedagogical philosophy we hold dear, the majority of us spend

DOI: 10.7330/9781646420315.c003

hours every semester reviewing, evaluating, and grading student writing. Furthermore, when course grades are added to student transcripts, they come to symbolize all the careful work accomplished over the term. Grades are the bottom line, and whether we want to admit it or not, grades are culturally powerful and ideologically charged. Perhaps nothing symbolizes education, especially in the United States, more than an A, B, C, D, or F. These symbols circulate throughout culture as points of pride and shame. Make no mistake, grades are punitive judgments that measure and rank students and eventually allow or disallow entrance to certain networks of power: advanced classes, graduation, interviews, government offices (Jensen 2010, 104–5). Grades are rhetorical texts that construct students not only for audiences in and outside the university but also for the students themselves (Carbone and Daisley 1998). Likewise, teachers and academic institutions are made and unmade by grades: programs grow or wither, retention and graduation rates rise or fall, state funding is received or withheld.

With so much embedded in the red marks left on student work and printed on academic transcripts, it isn't surprising most teachers search for "best practices" when grading writing. However, with scholarly attention focused elsewhere, two often entangled attitudes about grading emerge: an anxiety about grading ("Am I doing something wrong?" "Am I being too harsh?") and a feeling of power and privilege ("I refuse to give up my rigor!" "I know what an A paper looks like!"). These attitudes are symptomatic of a surveillance culture perpetuated through grades and grading practices, and, as I argue, intensified in an age of big data analytics where grades become important data points for predicting student "success." While other chapters in this collection focus on corporate surveillance or surveillance mechanisms inside websites and apps, this chapter joins Colleen Reilly's and Jenae Cohn, Norah Fahim, and John Peterson's chapters in addressing issues of surveillance and education. This chapter, however, is not an attempt to offer advice on grading or soothe anxieties; instead, I address issues of power and control embedded in grading, as well as the methodologies that use grades to build and reify neoliberal educational infrastructures.[1]

Teaching and grading writing are particularly useful when attempting to "professionalize" students. Richard Boyd (1998) and Ryan Skinnell (2016) remind us that the teaching of writing has been central to academic professionalization ever since the introduction of freshman composition at Harvard in 1885. Framed as objective measures, rigid grading schemes claim schools can sort people with precision (Schneider and Hutt 2013, 12); however, grading writing has always proven particularly difficult and exceptionally subjective (Copeland 1901, 76). It is not an overstatement, then, to say that early twentieth-century writing pedagogy's focus on grammatical and mechanical correctness was inspired, in part, by an attempt to make grading more objective. Even so, critics note grades' lack objectivity, pedagogical limitations, and negative influence on student's futures both in school (i.e., scholarships, matriculation, graduation) and out of school (i.e., employment opportunities). Educators should consider how a system that represents the messiness of learning in a singular symbol might alter students' desire to learn and teachers' ability to teach.

Within writing studies, discussions of grading have, for the most part, been sidestepped in favor of writing process(es), with most pedagogies advocating the deferment of judgement while students draft, revise, and reflect on their writing in collaboration with peers and instructors. However, even with deferred judgement, a grade must be assigned for students to proceed (or not) through the educational pipeline (Gale 1997). Stephen Tchudi (1997) explains grading as "one-dimensional, rewards/punishments, rank ordering, not descriptive, a priori criteria, future directed, one-symbol summative" (xiii) while Pat Belanoff famously calls grading "the dirty thing we have to do in the dark of our own offices" (1991, 61). Those who have taken on the issue of grading writing have sought to offer alternatives, such as contracts, rubrics, badges, and ePortfolios that merely redefine the terms without fundamentally challenging or changing grading ideologies (Haswell 1999). "Nevertheless,"

Peter Elbow laments, "we have an intractable dilemma: that grading is unfair and counterproductive but that students and institutions tend to want grades" (1993, 193).

The general thesis of this chapter argues that grades are an imperfect system of communication and corrupt technology of surveillance that serve a neoliberal university that values control, individualism, and financial gains above the critical, creative, and rhetorical education of its students. I argue surveillance happens at multiple levels during grading processes. First, at the local level, teachers surveil students in class and, through a complex network of observations and choices, assign a grade based on the student's ability to meet course goals and outcomes. Therefore, at the local level, grades are the *product of surveillance*. Second, on a larger scale, various stakeholders (administrators, university donors, state legislators, potential employers) surveil students, teachers, and their respective institutions through grades and grading trends. At this level, grades more damningly betray the complexity of teaching writing in favor of a false sense of objectivity and therefore are part of the *process of surveillance*. In what follows, I deploy theories of panoptic power and normalization to situate our understanding of grades within the discourses of surveillance. Building on Michel Foucault's argument about the intensification of power (1975) as well as Gilles Deleuze's theorization of control societies (1992), I address current discussions of big data/learning analytics in writing studies to suggest that this "change in scope" necessitates further questions about surveillance and grades as big data. Finally, I offer an ethics of care to work from underneath to uproot and disidentify from grading ideologies. We must, I conclude, undertake careful conversations about grades as a technology of surveillance in order to resist cultures of educational accountability and ubiquitous surveillance.

THE PANOPTIC GRADEBOOK

Grading is a technology of surveillance. Though the reviewed scholarship never situates grading as such, the talk of ranking, tracking, morality, and efficiency that animates grading ideologies is unquestionably one of surveillance. Indeed, if, as Selena Nemorin suggests, surveillance has been rearticulated as key to educational efficiency (2017), we must view teachers grading student products and productivity as surveillance. The concept of panoptic surveillance (Foucault 1975) helps us recognize grading practices as integral to the construction of educational infrastructures that operate invisibly and automatically to normalize and produce docile bodies.

For example, consider the teacher's gradebook as a panoptic technology. Whether a physical book or a record housed in an online learning-management system (LMS), the teacher can collectively observe students while tracking individual progress towards normalization. Gradebook data represent various disciplinary attempts insofar as student grades signal adherence or deviation from expected norms. With many writing norms based linked to colonial ideals of order, logic, masculinity, and racial privilege (see Mignolo 2011), students often compose linear academic arguments in Standard White American English. These norms, shielded by cultural hierarchies and writing infrastructures, are valued over nonacademic literacy practices specifically for their ability to reach and discipline mass audiences while intersectional and culturally sustaining ways of knowing are tokenized through neoliberal logics of "diversity" (Ahmed 2012).

Under these conditions, when an essay earns an A, the student is normalized and made more docile. The A student is rewarded for performing the tasks set, which often reify the institutionally mandated writing norms. Accordingly, lower grades require additional discipline, which may involve increased surveillance ("Come to my office hours to discuss how to improve your writing") or perhaps a threat of failure ("If you don't improve, you'll fail this course and your GPA will suffer"). This diminishes a student's position within networks of power. By impacting a student's understanding of self (Belanoff 1998; Main and Ost 2014; Yancey and Huot 1998), grades are excellent tools to discipline the body through the soul. The tracking of student "progress" via grades and other educational records propagated by administrative bodies as "objective" makes possible expansive cultures of surveillance and discipline. Regardless of the fact that many educator-activists problematize the concept of grade objectivity, power and privilege continuously circulate through grades. Discourses of objectivity, perhaps, are maintained through the teaching of writing itself, which disciplines students by demanding rationality, logic, and proper language use. Furthermore, as a near-universal requirement, writing classrooms are ideal surveillance sites. Skinnell supports this point by suggesting that "[the first-year writing course's] enduring existence in American higher education can be usefully understood by considering its positive value for meeting specific institutional needs irrespective of student needs, demographics, disciplinary knowledge, pedagogical best practices, or even improved student writing" (2016, 17).

Some may argue against this cynical view of the teaching of writing—it certainly gives me pause. After all, through writing, students access networks of power that can lead to economic success, cultural capital, and identity realization. However, the power accessed by students through institutionally approved writing is tempered by and often contingent on earning grades by following normalizing "learning outcomes" and "course goals" (Gallagher 2016). Our development and enforcement of such norms surveil, discipline, and punish students, especially students from communities who have not been normalized before entering the panoptic space of the writing classroom (Inoue 2014, 2019). There is no opportunity for exploration or productive failure. Grades, therefore, are a product of surveillance that circulate and maintain privileged infrastructures of writing. Weaponized as a technology of surveillance, grades communicate neoliberal values that construct students not only for audiences in and beyond the university but also for the students themselves. The process follows this path: grades label students ("this is an A student, that student is at risk of failing"), students perform identities based on those labels ("I'm smart" or "I'm stupid"), and students operate within material and cultural structures of power as determined by their identities (business executives, middle-class workers, and lower-class laborers).

A CHANGE OF SCALE: GRADES AS BIG DATA

Foucault notes as power becomes lighter, it intensifies, and the intensification of power drives its efficiency and growth while subtly coercing people (Foucault 1975, 209). The supposed objectivity and mobility of grades ensure that even as students move from one educational enclosure to another, they can be surveilled effectively. Furthermore, growing educational infrastructures require enhanced surveillance technologies and, thus, a "change of scale" (Foucault 1975, 142) in the assignment and collection of grades. And while grades are generated from local surveillance (teachers surveilling students), they also join other data points to facilitate the surveillance of students, teachers, and educational programs by various stakeholders. With grades (the product of earlier surveillance) being used within the process of larger-scale surveillance projects, they outgrow the panoptic metaphor and evolve into what Deleuze (1992) understands as technologies of control.

The shift from disciplinary societies (as theorized by Foucault) to societies of control (as theorized by Deleuze) is necessary when examining the contemporary university and its use of grades because the goal is no longer simple normalization but rather control. To this end, Nemorin argues we have entered an age of postpanoptic pedagogy, explaining: "As an extension on the characteristics of panoptic modes, surveillance in schools seemed to be moving from fixity to mobility. So, while panoptic models are certainly useful for mapping the ontologies of surveillance in school, the increasing digitization of such environments has changed the form and practice of surveillance in terms of muddying boundaries of time and space, physical and immaterial, public and private" (2017, 245). Nemorin's point builds from Deleuze's suggestion that control is a "new monster" that exists outside disciplinary enclosures: while bodies are made docile within enclosures, they must be controlled as they continuously circulate through various modulations. In control societies, "one is never finished with anything—the corporation, the educational system, the armed services being metastable states coexisting in one and the same modulation, like a universal system of deformation" (Deleuze 1992, 5). Writing programs and their home institutions are part of control societies, and grades become data points within massive data sets that control through "the systematic monitoring of individuals and/or groups through personal data networks in order to regulate or govern behaviours" (Nemorin 2017, 248), or dataveillance.

As writing programs grow more complex, some teaching dozens of sections to thousands of students every semester, the ability to surveil both teachers and students becomes more difficult, thus making way for dataveillance vis-á-vis big-data methodologies. The boom in big data analytics,[2] and the subfield of writing analytics, promises more accurate and "objective" information about writing programs through large-scale data collection, storage, and analysis. Mark Andrejevic and Kelly Gates suggest that big data allows new forms of "sense-making" (2014, 186), which is often understood, at least in higher education, as a predictive methodology. Writing scholars Susan Lang and Craig Baehr note, "One of the key features that separates the process of data or text mining from other statistical methods . . . is that the knowledge to be gained is implicit in the data. Data mining might be predictive, in that it seeks to forecast future actions or behaviors through examining patterns in the data, or descriptive, in that it attempts to explain those patterns and the implications thereof" (2012, 177–78). Such data—including grades, grading trends, and millions of other data points—can be used to various ends: assessment, programmatic revision, student intervention, scholarly research, and/or administrative review. Marc Scott succinctly explains big data's value to the teaching of writing and student retention when he writes, "For WPAs, having access to [big data analytics] could mean the ability to create more persuasive arguments that persuade stakeholders" (2017, 58). However, as with grades, the localized labor of writing pedagogy is abstracted by the spectacular bigness of data. As Linda Adler-Kassner suggests in her CCCC chair's address, "As [big data analytics] seek[s] to make granular this process, the choices students make, and the work of teaching, they also disassemble the rich and meaty ways in which writing is never just writing" (2017, 329). In short, big data analytics, especially in writing studies, is an exciting methodology to some that raises concern for others.

Advocates position big data analytics in terms of reliability, objectivity, and possibility—a truly optimistic rhetoric of technology (Hawisher and Selfe 1991). However, big data analytics has also been criticized as the latest surveillance technology. danah boyd and Kate Crawford present six critical points about big data: it changes the definition of knowledge (2012, 665); its claims to objectivity and accuracy are misleading (666); bigger data are not always better data (668); taken out of context, big data loses its meaning (670); its accessibility does not make it ethical (671); limited access to big data creates new digital divides (673). These points are echoed throughout the special issue "Big Data Surveillance" of *Surveillance and Society* in which Tyler Reigeluth argues big data analytics is not a radical departure from existing forms of surveillance and subjectivation but rather an intensification of existing networks of power and control (2014). This intensification helps support growing demands from various stakeholders. Again, as power becomes lighter, it intensifies, and the intensification of power drives its efficiency and growth while also abstracting its actions.

As writing scholars and multinational corporations develop technology-driven writing infrastructures to collect, analyze, and archive millions of student data points, we must closely examine the practices enacted in the name of innovation and accountability. We must also follow the data trail to find the source of the data that influences a growing range of important decisions. Following this trail, I believe, will often lead us back to grades and all their problems. Remember, grades both produce surveillance and contribute to larger-scale processes of surveillance.

WHEN BIG DATA MEETS WRITING STUDIES

With writing analytic technologies being developed by the likes of Pearson Publishing (Turnitin and MyCompLab), MacMillan Learning (WriterKey), Michigan State University (Eli Review), The Ohio State University (Writer's Exchange), and the University of South Florida (MyReviewers), it is important we question the motivations of such technologies, critique their enabling of surveillance, and think critically and creatively about how to use these technologies without negatively impacting students, teachers, programs, or communities (Beck et al. 2016). To maintain my focus on grades as a technology of surveillance, I signpost two goals for this section: (1) demonstrate how grades and grading trends have been used as big data in writing studies and (2) highlight the importance of conscience and control to make data valuable. To illustrate my points, I use the former first-year writing program at Texas Tech University (TTU) as my example.[3] While the programs (ICON) and LMS (TOPIC then RaiderWriter) are no longer in service,[4] for over fifteen years TTU utilized a big data analytics methodology to drive its pedagogical initiatives. Even with the controversy sparked by the program, it is hard to deny it jumpstarted the current writing analytics trend.

The radical redesign of the TTU program emerged from financial and logistical issues. The solution, a pedagogical model called Interactive Composition Online (ICON), launched in 2002, reduced face-to-face instruction time from 160 minutes to 80 minutes per week and raised the class cap from twenty-five students to thirty-five students per class (Wasley 2006) while implementing an in-house-designed learning-management and data-collection system (first TOPIC and then RaiderWriter). LMS collected and distributed all student work, including preliminary drafts, final drafts, peer critiques, portfolio reflections, and writing reviews, to a pool of "document instructors" who graded anonymously, while content was taught by "classroom instructors" (Hester 2007). This distributed grading model was central to ICON, and the influx of grades and instructor feedback provided "mounds of immediate data on student and instructor outputs" (Scott 2009, 181).

A managerial ideology coupled with these infrastructural changes sought to reduce supposed teacher subjectivity and radically different student learning experiences (Lang 2005). Fred Kemp, the former WPA and ICON creator, explained, "'We are not grading the writer; we are grading the writing. . . . No longer can a student earn good marks by buttering up the instructor. Teachers can't inflate the grade of a student who turns in consistently poor work just because he or she is deemed to be trying hard'" (Wasley 2006). The separation of grading from instruction, at face value, seems beneficial to the learning process; however, the multiplication of feedback and grades (with each piece of work graded by multiple document instructors) also conveniently serves the big data analytics methodology.

TTU, using ICON and RaiderWriter, created an archive of over two million pieces of graded student writing. Mining this data for various trends, including grading trends, allowed for what Susan Lang (2016, 2019), former TTU WPA and creator of RaiderWriter, calls an "agile methodology," which purportedly improves instruction in real time through the WPA's intervention in the grading trends, feedback loops, and the learning process in general. This on-demand-style curricular revision, Lang argues, is the most effective way to maintain program standards, increase student success, and reach institutional retention and graduation goals, or, put into conversation with my earlier points, effect a change in scale of surveillance and control. As much is clear in E. Jonathan Arnett and Lang's published longitudinal study of grading trends, which used a sample of thirty-eight thousand grades on three assignments between 2010 and 2014 to discern differences in grading patterns among three different teaching cohorts (lecturers with only MAs, lecturers with PhDs, and MA-PhD students) (2015, 220). And while their data show "little cause for programmatic alarm," Arnett and Lang suggest that "the WPA could institute a more focused review of particular assignments and *intensify norming sessions* prior to grading those assignments" (225–26; emphasis added). These "potential action items" are examples of grades and big data analytics informing the disciplinary actions designed to control instructors' normalization of students while also creating a perpetual cycle of data collection and analysis.

The TTU example, for me, demonstrates three concerning actions. First, the use of grades as an objective measure to build or revise curriculum limited pedagogical creativity and demonstrates that the grade is the goal. For students, writing and learning driven by grades is shallow. For teachers, the anxiety of reaching grade-distribution expectations (even if unstated) deeply affects effectiveness. For administrators and other stakeholders, grade data obscure the learning process, which is complex, individual, and messy, by presenting it as a single alphabetic symbol. Second, the issue of collection, analysis, and ownership of data should raise concerns. As Joseph Moxley explains, in TTU's ICON program, "agency resides more in the hands of the Writing Program Administrator and his colleagues who define the curriculum [based on the collected data]" (2008, 190). By controlling and continuously analyzing the "locally stored" data from which adjustments to standardized curriculum can be devised (Lang 2019; Lang and Gouge 2010), the WPA benefited from technologies of surveillance, like grades, and communities of power.[5] Third, TTU's pedagogy and data-collection method relied on consensus in order to make data meaningful, and grades are easily counted data points. Consensus in education often equates to normalization of some and marginalization of others. Furthermore, various interpretations of writing are what strengthen, not weaken, the teaching of writing. And while I'm not outright condemning the former TTU program or other writing-analytics practitioners, I return to the question of grades as big data. TTU's RaiderWriter system was an intentionally designed digital writing infrastructure that allowed its WPAs to track short-term patterns that might suggest immediate action (e.g., lackluster feedback on student work, unexpected grade changes, plagiarism) (Hudson and Lang 2013, 48–49; Lang 2019), as well as long-term action items (e.g., large-scale grading-trend analysis). One point on which Lang (2019) and I are in agreement is that WPAs should be active and vocal about the integration of technologies into our local writing infrastructures instead of being placed outside the institution's processes. But we don't have to play the institution's game. Afterall, how does theorizing student learning through the dual lens of failure and control advance the study and teaching of writing?

We, as teachers of writing, must ask ourselves very difficult questions concerning what student data is collected and how, how those data are used for programmatic change and/or scholarship, and whether our long-held pedagogical principles are still accomplishable under a dataveillance program. Linda Adler-Kassner, Heidi Estrem, Susan Miller-Cochran, Dawn Shepherd, and Elizabeth Wardle offer "savvy WPAs" a strong list of ethical questions to consider when contemplating the use of big data analytics in administrative decisions. Key questions are, "How is the data used? To target those deemed at risk for help and intervention? Or is [*sic*] the data used to guide action that might lead to a pernicious feedback loop that it helps sustain? Is it a model that profiles people by their circumstances that then helps create the environment that justifies assumptions about those people? Does this system just codify the past, or does it attempt to make changes for the future?" (2017). Such questions caution us not to reinscribe dangerous ideologies in the name of technological innovation or institutional accountability.

Too often grades and big data analytics are used to verify students as "at risk" without exploring the localized conditions and problematic ideologies that label them as such. Christina Cedillo, in this collection, discusses dataveillance and data segmentation, and grades are a manageable data set that can be circulated to signify "the student," "the teacher," "the learning experience." The patterns mined from grades tell an extremely limited story about those who are normalized, those who need further discipline, and those in control. Grades, therefore, contribute to the "identity-avoidant frameworks" Cedillo theorizes by constructing student and teacher identities that either permit or restrict social, material, and cultural resources.

AN ETHICS OF CARE

Using grade data, regardless of size, is telling an incomplete story. At the individual level, grades, at best, are a representation of a student's ability to satisfy the norms set for an assignment, and, on more global scales, grading trends demonstrate very little in terms of critical, creative, and rhetorical learning. Even the best curriculum carefully negotiated with ethical intentions by skilled students, teachers, and administrators is abstracted to outside stakeholders when solely represented by grades. At larger scales, the careful work of complex writing pedagogies is rendered nearly invisible by the symbolic A, B, C, D, or F when entangled with millions of other data points. Unfortunately, grades are a function of contemporary education, and consequently, we are all implicated through our use of grades. Indeed, grades facilitate multidirectional surveillance, with teachers surveilling students, administrators surveilling teachers, students surveilling programs, outside stakeholders surveilling institutions, and any combination thereof. In a surveillance society, no one is innocent. But resistance is possible and necessary. Indeed, Black, Indigenous, feminist, queer, and decolonial thought help us strategically come from underneath and disidentify from grading and cultures of surveillance by "working on and against" them (Muñoz 1999, 11–12). By way of conclusion, I offer this ethics of care for teachers, students, and administrators to encourage us to "more explicitly acknowledge the unequal and asymmetrical power relations and commit [ourselves] to being transparent regarding [our] intentions and processes" (Prinsloo and Slade 2017, 117).[6] This ethics of care cannot dismantle grading and big-data infrastructures identified in this chapter, but it offers a way for us to care for each other while the slow work of change comes from underneath through "small potent gestures" (Selfe 1999).

First, recognize that the work of normalization, which we all participate in as educators, leads to extensive ethical problems as opposed to the promised utopia. In understanding that no standard system of evaluation, especially something as reductionist as assigning grades, can address the complexity of writing and its interrelated practices, we must recommit to serving our local communities and their needs. Specifically, we must work with students, program administrators, and other stakeholders to demystify grading practices, counter discourses of objectivity, and make clear through action that grading is distinct from the learning process. Strong examples of this work include Asao B. Inoue's labor-based grading contracts (2019), Jesse Stommel (2018) and Susan D. Blum's respective work on ungrading (2020), and my own ruminations on a cultural rhetorics framework for assessment (Johnson 2020). Understanding how we signify failure and success in contemporary writing infrastructures is key to working on and against technologies of surveillance, normalization, and control, and we must do more work to not only identify these technologies of surveillance (as I have done here) but also delink our practices from the ideologies of colonial, Western Modernity (Mignolo 2011).

Second, understand that student data belong to students and treat those data with care and respect. It is ethically unsound for university bodies to claim ownership over educational data, and we must hold accountable institutions who collect data for disciplinary and normalizing purposes. Furthermore, we must be sure any and all data collected, reviewed, and used for program development or scholarship are collected in an ethical way. At all levels, we must be open and honest about our data-collection methods, storage, analysis, and use. No longer can we hide behind the notion that bare minimal permissions and promises of anonymity constitute ethical data collection. Data, even data believed to be scrubbed, leave a trail that points to their creator (Daniel 2017, 2). Without taking the utmost care with their data, we are placing students and colleagues in danger. Furthermore, by centering anonymity as our only ethical option, we position the patterns found and formed via big data analytics as "self-evident" and, thus, justify pedagogical changes or disciplinary measures ignorant of (or, worst, in spite of) localized and culturally specific considerations. Our material and embodied needs as learners and educators cannot be lost in the bigness of the data.

Finally, continue to work on and against the neoliberal structures that use power to discipline students, teachers, and so
many other communities. By working with stakeholders and
policy makers to explain the problems with current models
of education, limitations of big data analytics, and the harmful nature of grades, we can reorient power so it works to our
benefit rather than our oppression. The "knowledge of crowds"
Moxley (2008) reminds us, creates communities of learning
rather than communities of power. This sentiment echoes the
important and ongoing work of coalition demanded by Black,
Ingenious people of color (BIPOC) as well as queer, trans, and
disabled communities.[7] And while changing our grading practices and conducting our research through an ethics of care
will not demolish the neoliberal university or other oppressive power structures, it is through these "small potent gestures" that we can refuse normalization and counteract surveillance technologies.

ACKNOWLEDGEMENTS

I offer sincere gratitude to Scott DeWitt, Michael Faris, Ryan
Sheehan, and my reviewers for their feedback on earlier drafts.
I'm also grateful for Estee's and Les's patience and kindness as
editors and mentors throughout this process. Finally, thank you
to Chris Anson and Susan Miller-Cochran for planting the earliest seeds of this project years ago in their WPA seminar.

NOTES

1. Since drafting the first versions of this chapter, I have shifted many of
   citational commitments to be more attentive to the scholarship of BIPOC
   and the necessary work of decolonization and relational knowledge
   making. I have purposefully made inroads, especially in the concluding
   section, for future research that takes on the ethical commitments of
   cultural rhetorics.
2. *Big data analytics* is an umbrella term for a variety of technologies that
   collect and archive large-scale data sets that cannot be analyzed without
   technological assistance. Some of the authors I cite may use alternate
   terms, and I have kept their original language in direct citations.

3. The first-year writing program at TTU has been discussed at length by
    Gouge (2009); Hester, (2007); Kemp (2005); Lang (2005, 2016); Lang
    and Baehr (2012); Moxley (2008); Rickly (2006); Scott (2009); and
    Wasley (2006).
4. At the time of this writing, the first-year writing program at TTU is under-
    going a radical change in curriculum and programmatic philosophy.
    The pilot program completely dismantles RaiderWriter and the big data
    analytics-driven pedagogy of ICON.
5. Moxley (2008) defines "Communities of Power" in opposition to
    "Communities of Learning": "Communities of Learning thrive on col-
    laboration and distributed power whereas Communities of Power are less
    interactive, more autocratically controlled" (183).
6. While the phrase "ethics of care" may evoke specific meaning in the care
    ethics community and Prinsloo and Slade work within that meaning in
    their scholarship, I use this term in this chapter broadly to encompass a
    constellation of practices for ethics of care within many communities.
7. My praxis is deeply influenced by the work of BIPOC, queer, feminist,
    and disability scholar-activists such as Karma Chávez (2013), María
    Lugones (2003), Natasha Jones (2020), Audre Lorde (1984), and many
    others.

REFERENCES

Adler-Kassner, Linda. 2017. "2017 CCCC Chair's Address: Because Writing Is
    Never Just Writing." *College Composition and Communication* 69 (2): 317–40.
Adler-Kassner, Linda, Heidi Estrem, Susan Miller-Cochran, Dawn Shepherd,
    and Elizabeth Wardle. 2017. "The WPA's Guide to Data Analytics: Predictive,
    Data, and Learning." Presentation at the annual Conference of Writing
    Program Administrators, Knoxville, TN, July 20–23.
Ahmed, Sara. 2012. *On Being Included: Racism and Diversity in Institutional Life.*
    Durham, NC: Duke University Press.
Andrejevic, Mark, and Kelly Gates. 2014. "Big Data Surveillance: Introduction."
    Surveillance & Society 12 (2): 185–96. http://ojs.library.queensu.ca/index
    .php/surveillance-and-society/article/view/5242.
Arnett, E. Jonathan, and Susan Lang. 2015. "'Mirror, Mirror . . .' Who's the
    Fairest of Them All?: A Longitudinal Assessment of FYC Instructors' Grading
    Trends." In *Beyond the Frontier: Innovations in First-Year Composition,* edited by
    Jill Dahlman and Piper Seldon, 218–33. Cambridge: Cambridge Scholars.
Beck, Estee N., Angela Crow, Heidi A. McKee, Colleen A. Reilly, Jennifer
    deWinter, Stephanie Vie, Laura Gonzales, and Dànielle Nicole DeVoss. 2016.
    "Writing in an Age of Surveillance, Privacy, and Net Neutrality." *Kairos: A
    Journal of Rhetoric, Technology, and Pedagogy* 20 (2). kairos.technorhetoric.net
    /20.2/topoi/beck-et-al/crow.html.
Belanoff, Pat. 1991. "The Myths of Assessment." *Journal of Basic Writing* 10 (1):
    54–66.

Belanoff, Pat. 1998. "Toward an Ethics of Grading." In *Foregrounding Ethical Awareness in Composition and English Studies*, edited by Sheryl I. Fontaine and Susan M. Hunter, 174–96. Portsmouth, NH: Boynton/Cook.

Blum, Susan D., ed. 2020. *Ungrading: Why Rating Students Undermines Learning (and What to Do Instead)*. Morgantown: West Virginia University Press.

boyd, danah, and Kate Crawford. 2012. "Critical Questions for Big Data." *Information, Communication & Society* 15 (5): 37–41. doi:10.1080/136911 8X.2012.678878.

Boyd, Richard. 1998. "The Origins and Evolution of Grading Student Writing: Pedagogical Imperatives and Cultural Anxieties." In *The Theory and Practice of Grading Writing: Problems and Possibilities*, edited by Frances Zak and Christopher C. Weaver, 3–16. Albany: SUNY Press.

Carbone, Nick, and Margaret Daisley. 1998. "Grading as a Rhetorical Construct." In *The Theory and Practice of Grading Writing: Problems and Possibilities*, edited by Frances Zak and Christopher C. Weaver, 77–94. Albany: SUNY Press.

Chávez, Karma R. 2013. *Queer Migration Politics: Activist Rhetoric and Coalitional Possibilities*. Champaign: University of Illinois Press.

Copeland, C. T. 1901. *Freshman English and Theme-Correcting in Harvard College*. New York: Silver, Burdett.

Daniel, Ben Kei, ed. 2017. *Big Data and Learning Analytics in Higher Education*. New York: Springer. doi:10.1007/978-3-319-06520-5.

Deleuze, Gilles. 1992. "Postscript on the Societies of Control." *October* 59: 3–7.

Elbow, Peter. 1993. "Ranking, Evaluating, and Liking: Sorting Out Three Forms of Judgment." *College English* 55 (2): 187–206.

Foucault, Michel. 1975. *Discipline and Punish: The Birth of the Prison*. New York: Vintage Books.

Gale, Xi Liu. 1997. "Judgment Deferred: Reconsidering Institutional Authority in the Portfolio Writing Classroom." In *Grading in the Post-Process Classroom: From Theory to Practice*, edited by Libby Allison, Lizbeth Bryant, and Maureen Hourigan, 75–93. Portsmouth, NH: Boynton/Cook.

Gallagher, Chris W. 2016. "Our Trojan Horse: Outcomes Assessment and the Resurrection of Competency-Based Education." In *Composition in the Age of Austerity*, edited by Nancy Welch and Tony Scott, 21–34. Logan: Utah State University Press.

Gouge, Catherine. 2009. "Conversations at a Crucial Moment: Hybrid Courses and the Future of Writing Programs." *College English* 71 (4): 338–62.

Haswell, Richard H. 1999. "Grades, Time, and the Curse of Course." *College Composition and Communication* 51 (2): 284–95.

Hawisher, Gail E, and Cynthia L. Selfe. 1991. "The Rhetoric of Technology and the Electronic Writing Class." *College Composition and Communication* 42 (1): 55–65. doi:10.2307/357539.

Hester, Vicki. 2007. "When Pragmatics Precede Pedagogy." *Journal of Writing Assessment* 3 (2): 123–44. http://journalofwritingassessment.org/archives/3 -2.4.pdf.

Hudson, Robert, and Susan M. Lang. 2013. "Redevelop, Redesign, and Refine: Expanding the Functionality and Scope of TTOPIC into Raider Writer." In *Designing Web-Based Applications for 21st Century Writing Classrooms*, edited by George Pullman and Baotong Gu, 37–49. Amityville, NY: Baywood Press.

Inoue, Asao B. 2014. "Theorizing Failure in U.S. Writing Assessments." *Research in the Teaching of English* 48 (3): 330–52.

Inoue, Asao B. 2019. *Labor-Based Grading Contracts: Building Equity and Inclusion in the Compassionate Writing Classroom.* Fort Collins, CO: WAC Clearinghouse.

Jensen, Kyle. 2010. "The Panoptic Portfolio: Reassessing Power in Process-Oriented Writing Instruction." *JAC* 30 (1/2): 95–141.

Johnson, Gavin P. 2020. "Considering the Possibilities of a Cultural Rhetorics Assessment Framework." *Constellations: A Cultural Rhetorics Publishing Space.* http://constell8cr.com/issue-3/considering-the-possibilities-of-a-cultural -rhetorics-assessment-framework/.

Jones, Natasha N. 2020. "Coalitional Learning in the Contact Zones: Inclusion and Narrative Inquiry in Technical Communication and Composition Studies." *College English* 82 (5): 515–26.

Kemp, Fred. 2005. "The Aesthetic Anvil: The Foundations of Resistance to Technology and Innovation in English Departments." In *Market Matters: Applied Rhetoric Studies and Free Market Competition,* edited by Locke Carter, 77–94. Cresskill, NJ: Hampton.

Lang, Susan. 2005. "New Process, New Product: Redistributing Labor in a First-Year Writing Program." In *Market Matters: Applied Rhetoric Studies and Free Market Competition,* edited by Locke Carter, 187–204. Cresskill, NJ: Hampton.

Lang, Susan M. 2016. "Taming Big Data through Agile Approaches to Instructor Training and Assessment: Managing Ongoing Professional Development in Large First-Year Writing Programs." *WPA: Writing Program Administration* 39 (2): 79–102.

Lang, Susan. 2019. "Writing Analytics for the Agile WPA." Paper presented at the 7th Annual International Conference on Writing Analytics, St. Petersburg, FL, January 25–26.

Lang, Susan, and Craig Baehr. 2012. "Data Mining: A Hybrid Methodology for Complex and Dynamic Research." *College Composition and Communication* 64 (1): 172–94.

Lang, Susan M., and Catherine Gouge. 2010. "Comment & Response: 'Conversation at a Critical Moment: Hybrid Courses and the Future of Writing Programs.'" *College English* 72 (5): 554–58.

Lorde, Audre. 1984. *Sister Outsider: Essays and Speeches.* Berkeley, CA: Crossing Press.

Lugones, María. 2003. *Pilgrimages/Peregrinajes: Theorizing Coalition against Multiple Oppressions.* Lanham, MD: Rowman & Littlefield Publishers.

Main, Joyce, and Ben Ost. 2014. "The Impact of Letter Grades on Student Effort, Course Selection, and Major Choice: A Regression-Discontinuity Analysis." *Journal of Economic Education* 45 (1): 1–10.

Mignolo, Walter D. 2011. *The Darker Side of Western Modernity: Global Futures, Decolonial Options.* Durham, NC: Duke University Press.

Moxley, Joseph. 2008. "Datagogies, Writing Spaces, and the Age of Peer Production." *Computers and Composition* 25 (2): 182–202.

Muñoz, José Esteban. 1999. *Disidentifcations: Queers of Color and the Performance of Politics.* Minneapolis: University of Minnesota Press.

Nemorin, Selena. 2017. "Post-Panoptic Pedagogies: The Changing Nature of School Surveillance in the Digital Age." *Surveillance & Society* 15 (2): 239–53.

Prinsloo, Paul, and Sharon Slade. 2017. "Big Data, Higher Education and Learning Analytics: Beyond Justice, towards an Ethics of Care." In *Big Data and Learning Analytics in Higher Education*, edited by Ben Kei Daniel, 109–24. New York: Springer.

Reigeluth, Tyler Butler. 2014. "Why Data Is Not Enough: Digital Traces as Control of Self and Self-Control." *Surveillance & Society* 12 (2): 243–54. http://ojs.library.queensu.ca/index.php/surveillance-and-society/article/view/4741.

Rickly, Rebecca. 2006. "Distributed Teaching, Distributed Learning: Integrating Technology and Criteria-Driven Assessment into the Delivery of First-Year Composition." In *Delivering College Composition: The Fifth Canon*, edited by Kathleen Blake Yancey, 183–98. Portsmouth: Boynton/Cook.

Schneider, Jack, and Ethan Hutt. 2013. "Making the Grade: A History of the A–F Marking Scheme." *Journal of Curriculum Studies* 46 (2): 1–24.

Scott, Marc. 2017. "Big Data and Writing Program Retention Assessment: What We Need to Know." In *Retention, Persistence, and Writing Programs*, edited by Todd Ruecker, Dawn Sheperd, Heidi Estrem, and Beth Brunk-Chavez, 56–73. Logan: Utah State University Press.

Scott, Tony. 2009. *Dangerous Writing: Understanding the Political Economy of Composition*. Logan: Utah State University Press.

Selfe, Cynthia L. 1999. *Technology and Literacy in the Twenty-First Century: The Importance of Paying Attention*. Carbondale: Southern Illinois University Press.

Skinnell, Ryan. 2016. *Conceding Composition: A Crooked History of Composition's Institutional Fortunes*. Logan: Utah State University Press.

Stommell, Jesse. 2018. "How to Ungrade." March 18, 2018. https://www.jessestommel.com/how-to-ungrade/.

Tchudi, Stephen. 1997. "Introduction: Degrees of Freedom in Assessment, Evaluation, and Grading." In *Alternatives to Grading Student Writing*, edited by Stephen Tchudi, ix–xvii. NCTE.

Wasley, Paula. 2006. "A New Way to Grade." *Chronicle of Higher Education* 52 (27): https://www.chronicle.com/article/a-new-way-to-grade/.

Yancey, Kathleen Blake, and Brian Huot. 1998. "Construction, Deconstruction, and (Over) Determination: A Foucaultian Analysis of Grades." In *The Theory and Practice of Grading Writing: Problems and Possibilities*, edited by Frances Zak and Christopher C. Weaver, 39–52. Albany: SUNY Press.

PART II

Surveillance and Bodies

4

DEEP CIRCULATION

Dustin Edwards

Circulation has become a key concept for theorizing writing and rhetoric in a digital age. While circulation research has added much to our theories and pedagogies, work remains in understanding how circulation is shaped and exploited by the increased surveillance capabilities of a digital age. The circulation of writing is routinely surveilled by commercial and governmental entities that have algorithmic discretion to collect, research, and sell our online movements (Beck 2015; Beck et al. 2016; McKee 2011; Reilly in this collection; Reyman 2013; Vie and Miller in this collection). Further, many everyday embodied practices are circulating without our explicit knowing in the form of digital data flows, participating in a deep ecology made up of data brokers, business strategies, proprietary algorithms, material infrastructures, and so on. In short, we know not (all) what we circulate.

In this chapter, I theorize such a condition as deep circulation, which I define as the multiplicity of flows produced through acts of embodied composing. Deep circulation articulates a move to understand circulation—its effects on cultures, communities, environments, and bodies—through overlapping and entangled senses of flow: the affective, the textual, and the infrastructural. Deep circulation, then, is not so much a naming of a new kind of circulation but a grappling with multiple flows all at once. According to the OED, "deep" signifies, in a literal sense, "having great or considerable extension" and, in a more figurative sense, "something that is hard to fathom." Both of these understandings are instructive for the kind of circulation I aim to mark in this chapter: noting multiple dimensionalities not always easy to perceive.

DOI: 10.7330/9781646420315.c004

In relation to surveillance, I argue deep circulation provides a framework for recognizing the value and vulnerability of circulation. Circulations of all kinds are vital for robust and meaningful rhetorical participation. Yet, the logic of circulation—of unbounded flows that travel throughout time and space—is central to conditions of "liquid surveillance" (Bauman and Lyon 2013), where surveillance is not bounded to particular locales but rather moves with people as they traverse everyday life. To circulate often means producing mobile flows that provide advanced opportunities for surveillance, which, in turn, sustain conditions of precarity for marginalized identities and bodies. In response, this chapter cautions against privileging any dimensionality of circulation over another; instead, we must grapple with the many circulations writing bodies carry as they traverse everyday life.

To explain how deep circulation plays out in everyday encounters, I examine the rather mundane practice of exercise at my local YMCA. In particular, I note how circulations—of bodies, texts, and data—are surveilled via a contracted health and fitness platform called Mywellness Cloud. In essence, Mywellness tracks the circulation of bodies by prompting gym members to log in to its platform as they move from machine to machine and further asks them to share updates on social media and the Mywellness online community. More than textual circulations of status updates, Mywellness also renders such movement into a kind of black-boxed circulatory capital that provides many stakeholders (local gym staff and management, corporate interests, and other third-party advertisers) with robust data profiles of users. In describing black-boxed circulatory capital, I draw attention to (a) the opaque manner in which information flows on this platform and (b) the inherent economic value of such information for the platform and third parties. Frank Pasquale describes a "black box" as a useful metaphor for understanding much of our modern surveillance practices: "Tracked ever more closely by firms and government, we have no clear idea of just how far much of this information can travel, how it is used, or its consequences" (2015, 3). Data flows extracted from bodies on fitness platforms are of particular value to health and pharmaceutical industries, insurance companies, and financial institutions (Lupton 2016). The desire to track the circulations of one's body is anything but a private affair: circulations radiate into obscure directions for myriad purposes.

This chapter begins by investigating the intersections between two distinct areas of inquiry in rhetoric and writing studies: circulation studies and surveillance studies. In particular, I describe how tenets of a deep-circulation framework—affective, textual, and infrastructural flows—can each participate in surveillance practices. Then, I more fully explicate the notion of deep circulation, suggesting that while bracketing flows into distinct categories can be helpful at a conceptual level, circulations are always much more entangled and therefore should be understood as deeply connected and intradependent. To assess how deep circulation operates, I then attempt to attune myself to the many circulations of my local YMCA and its use of fitness-tracking technology. I close by discussing how a deep-circulation framework can inform an ethical and political stance when composing in hypercirculatory—and hypersurveilled—spaces.

CIRCULATION MEETS SURVEILLANCE

Broadly, circulation names how texts, bodies, objects, affects, and so on move through time and space (Edwards 2017). Circulation studies (Gries 2013) has opened space to consider many of the goals of writing and rhetoric: it works to effect change (Gries 2015; Ridolfo and DeVoss 2009), sustain cultures and build publics (Ridolfo 2015; Trimbur 2000), and transmit affective intensities (Chaput 2010; Edbauer 2005). While circulation studies have gained much traction in rhetoric and writing, not much work has investigated the entanglement between circulation and surveillance practices. Consider, for example, the simple act of "sharing" content on social media. Sharing not only moves content throughout and across social media ecosystems but also moves personal data into streams collected by various third parties and institutions (Amidon and Reyman

2014). This splintering of circulation increasingly cannot be avoided—that is, textual circulation often carries divergent flows of data circulation, streams that can be sorted, valued, and recirculated yet again. Flows propagate more flows and quickly get out of reach, all moving at divergent dimensions and temporalities.

But the logic of surveilling circulatory flows goes much deeper than sharing media on digital platforms. In an age of wearable technology and always-on devices, a human body increasingly carries whole archives of opaque, yet valuable, flows of data. In surveillance cultures, as Irma van der Ploeg writes, "who you are, how you are, and how you are going to be treated in various situations is increasingly known to various agents and agencies through information deriving from your own body; information that is processed elsewhere, through the networks, databases, and algorithms of the information society" (2012, 177). Even those who are mindful of their data practices cannot fully escape this condition. As Judith Gregory and Geoffrey Bowker explain, data streams begin to circulate before birth, "circulat[ing] out of the unformed fetus" (2016, 213). These performative data streams are used to make medical decisions, and, if carried through to birth, extend beyond to have consequentiality in the child's life.

As such, surveillance and the diminishment of privacy—especially on corporate platforms—has become something of an accepted trade-off for services with connective power. After all, as David Lyon asserts, "Surveillance is not just practiced on us, we participate in it" (2015, 3). The acceptance of surveillance as a part of everyday life manifests in myriad ways on the social web: for example, when users allow platforms to "tag" photos of friends using biometric data and facial recognition; or when users click on advertisements or suggested posts; and when users allow platforms access to hardware and data streams on individual devices.

In addition to the normalization of surveillance, the increased liquidity of surveillance in all aspects of social life presents challenges for understanding where, how, and to what effects surveillance operates. Kevin Haggerty and Richard Ericson's understanding of the "surveillant assemblage" provides a view of the complexity at play here. For Haggerty and Ericson, the surveillant assemblage "operates by abstracting human bodies from their territorial settings and separating them into a series of discrete flows. These flows are then reassembled into distinct 'data doubles' which can be scrutinized and targeted for intervention" (2000, 606). The notion of "data doubles" suggests that vast archives of personalized information circulate absent the territorialized body, traveling via infrastructures subject to sorting, categorization, and other surveillance techniques. In other words, a multiplicity of circulatory flows is always being produced through everyday acts of composing, flows that can be aggregated, duplicated, sorted, and recirculated. Circulation, it might be said, is a precondition for surveillance as we know it today.

To orient our senses to circulatory multiplicities, I propose situating circulation as occurring at three distinct, though entangled, dimensionalities: the affective, the textual, and the infrastructural. Whereas the affective level would question how affective energies circulate in daily life, the textual level would investigate the production, consumption, and exchange of texts once delivered. The infrastructural level, which I believe has received the least amount of attention from rhetorical circulation studies, would seek to disclose the often-unacknowledged material structures on and with which circulatory flows travel. To attempt to hold these flows in productive tension—to consider a deep circulation—can be one way to contemplate how circulation is fraught with privacy and surveillance concerns.

Affective Circulation

Affective circulation names a dimensionality of circulation that can be easily felt but difficult to render into representation. Affect, understood here, can be thought of as a kind of surging pulse that moves through and among bodies of all kinds to accumulate, pass through, or gum up, provoking sensations, attachments, and intuitions as it circulates (Edwards and Lang 2018). Scholars have increasingly turned to affect to describe a kind of presymbolic intensity that circulates and energizes social and cultural spheres (e.g., Chaput 2010; Edbauer 2005). Affect, related but distinct from emotion, is often described as having generative force, provoking, inciting, overwhelming, or suspending as it circulates through everyday encounters.

Affect theory often looks at the multigenerative relationship among bodies and spaces (Ahmed 2004). Derek McCormack argues "bodies and spaces co-produce one another through practices, gestures, movements, and events" (2014, 2). In so doing, affective spaces are generated "whose qualities and consistencies are vague but sensed, albeit barely, as a distinctive affective tonality, mood, or atmosphere" (3). For McCormack, affective spaces can be managed, so to speak, through institutional design, architecture, and cultural practices; this is why we feel a kind of affective atmosphere in stadiums, in movie theaters, in classrooms, in social media spaces. The circulation of affect matters in spaces, digital or otherwise, because it comes to bear on what is possible—on the "'not yet' of a body's doing" (Seigworth and Gregg 2010, 4)—in any given encounter. Because affective spaces have such force, they can mobilize certain habits, trajectories, and practices. In effect, practices of "keeping count," self-tracking, monitoring, and so forth are normalized on affective registers.

Textual Circulation

Textual circulation names a dimension at the level of production, exchange, and consumption. While any notion of text or textuality is complex and difficult to define, I rely on Steven Mailloux's definition as a starting point: "By 'texts' I mean objects of interpretive attention, whether speech, writing, non-linguistic practices, or human artifacts of any kind" (2002, 98). Textual circulation describes how composed texts across genres and media enter networks of broader circulation once they are distributed in particular moments and venues—what Jim Ridolfo and Dànielle Nicole DeVoss call "rhetorical velocity" (2009). Textual circulation is often about contributing to (counter)public life and adding value to communities (e.g., Gries 2015; Hawk 2012; Ridolfo 2015; Trimbur 2000; Warner 2005).

However, to enter a text into public fields of circulation is to subject the text to conditions of surveillance. As Christina Cedillo explains in their chapter in this collection, the livelihood of an individual—not to mention their safety—can be risked once texts enter networks of circulation. Certainly, the threat of surveillance and the ways particular social media posts might be negatively appropriated by others can be incorporated into rhetorical velocity heuristics. And yet, attempting to strategize the possible uptake of social media posts—how texts may be retroactively tracked, traced, and followed—can be a potentially self-censoring activity.

Infrastructures of Circulation

The last dimensionality of circulation concerns itself with the often-unacknowledged infrastructures by, through, and with which information travels. In terms of new media production, infrastructures involve those visible and invisible structures that impinge upon and make possible networked communication (DeVoss, Cushman, and Grabill 2005). More than technical structures, infrastructures influence the relational—ethical—contours of networked life (Brown 2015). Infrastructures of circulation are dependent on what media theorists Lisa Parks and Nicole Starosielski call media infrastructures—"situated sociotechnical systems that are designed and configured to support the distribution of audiovisual signal traffic" (2015, 4). Thus, infrastructures of circulation point to the complex technical-material assemblages involved in carrying, ordering, and filtering flows of information.

Infrastructures of circulation are key for advanced surveillance operations today, as surveillance demands complex infrastructures to gather, collect, use, sell, and recirculate information with precision and speed. Encoded decisions are the

underlying infrastructure that provides conditions for automated and algorithmic surveillance. Such surveillance is made
capable through the collection, organization, and recirculation
of data sets. Data circulations have become critical nodes for
surveillance procedures, marking a distinct change from older
modes of surveillance to dataveillance. In addition, rather than
seeing data as ephemeral or immaterial sources of information,
paying attention to how data travel along material routes is
important for issues of surveillance (Parikka 2015).

DEEP CIRCULATION

Taken together, the three dimensions of circulation describe
a layered approach to studying and attending to circulation,
what I call *deep circulation*. To consider the movements of these
flows simultaneously—to attempt to hold them in productive
tension—is to consider a kind of deep circulation. Those who
participate in online activities (posting to Facebook, browsing
Amazon, searching Google) are producing deep flows of circulation. Those who move about their everyday lives with smartphones in their pockets/bags or wearable technologies on their
bodies are also producing deep flows of circulation. These flows
are derived from the human body but move at divergent rates
and scale up into forms of big data. As such, deep circulation
orients us to the multiple, to the duplicitous, to the splintering, to the fracturing. It looks at but also moves beyond visible
dimensionalities of perception and takes inroads into the non-
representational. It follows circulations as they faintly emerge,
as they get out of reach, as they diverge into multiple affective,
textual, and infrastructural registers.

Deep circulation reveals the inherent fraught relationship
between practices of circulation and procedures of surveillance.
On the one hand, the circulation of affect and texts—made
possible through material infrastructures—can do important
world-building and political work. Circulation can raise awareness, build affinities, and produce (counter)publics to effect
change. On the other hand, the very logic of circulation—of

information flows that move throughout time and space—sets the conditions of surveillance as we know them today. Deep circulation reminds us that multiplicities of circulation are necessarily difficult to trace out: circulations fracture and give way to new circulations. Human bodies turn to data bodies, affect turns to text turns to data, and on and on.

Considering the multiplicity of flows circulating at various scales and dimensionalities opens up space for many areas of inquiry within rhetoric and writing, and particularly within surveillance studies and circulation studies. I turn to one such trajectory in the next section. For my purpose here, I pay particular attention to how bodily movements are rendered into textual and data flows that move promiscuously via the opaque infrastructure of Mywellness Cloud.

DEEP CIRCULATION AT A YMCA

Gyms are spaces full of movement, and my local YMCA is no different. At the Y, people circulate around many spaces designed for exercise—cardio rooms, weight-training spaces, fitness classrooms, pools, basketball and racquetball courts, and so on. The Y is an affective space. It is full of sharpened and dulled tonalities and atmospheres where bodies, objects, signs, and spaces coalesce to throw together a world (McNely 2016; Stewart 2011). There's a kind of energy that moves throughout the space, one that buzzes especially during peak hours and flattens during slow times. The world at the YMCA moves and changes with a kind of circulatory intensity (McNely 2016), which is not mere a backdrop to the space but is an intensity that readies bodies for other kinds of circulations and presents conditions capable of normalizing certain practices, behaviors, and routines.

Bodies move, bodies keep count. At the Y, television monitors display fitness accomplishments from patrons who record and display their movements for other gym goers to see. Miles run, steps taken, pounds lifted, calories expended—all are aggregated into a digital "leaderboard" that displays the day's top fitness performers. In the age of self-tracking and the Quantified

Self (Lupton 2016; Neff and Nafus 2016), the logging and circulating of forms of biodata has become something of a mundane practice. Health and fitness trackers collect data and link up with social media networks to circulate textual updates of major accomplishments that then travel on vast infrastructures into data centers all over the globe. Share your run. Share your workout. Share your progress. Move and let your data move.

At my particular Y, the promoted way to keep count is through Mywellness Cloud, which is readily seen throughout the gym. In addition to monitors displaying movements of those sharing their exercising profiles, an invitation to sign up for Mywellness begins when signing up for a Y membership. Patrons are also reminded of Mywellness when beginning a workout on most stationary cardio machines and on signage posted throughout the gym. In simple terms, Mywellness Cloud is a database that logs, organizes, and shares personal data. But, as described next, a quick detour into its corporate structure, terms of use, and data policies reveals more complexity behind this database.

The Mywellness Cloud platform is owned and operated by TechnoGym, an international company headquartered in Cesena, Italy. According to the company website, TechnoGym caters to a range of small- to large-scale health and fitness operations, selling equipment and services to commercial gyms, cruise ships, and medical centers. Globally, TechnoGym claims that more than thirty-five million people use its equipment daily (TechnoGym 2017b). In addition to manufacturing and selling fitness equipment, TechnoGym also touts itself as an overall "wellness" provider. Mywellness Cloud, which contracts with fitness centers around the world, is designed to move beyond the gym. That is, according to the terms of use policy, Mywellness aims to create a personal experience "on the move" (a phrase often used in the company's branding)—as users can access their data via web browsers and mobile and tablet applications. The "service" Mywellness provides, according to its terms of use, is twofold: the platform (1) "stores, organizes, and processes data . . . within a database that can be accessed remotely through the Website or from a mobile device" and (2) "organizes personalized exercise sessions or sports competitions and uses multimedia content" (TechnoGym 2017b).

To more clearly understand the Mywellness Cloud platform, it's helpful to see how its branding appeals to everyday users, on the one hand, and the fitness industry on the other. Everyday users, as stated in the terms of use and seen elsewhere on its website and mobile app interfaces, can track their health and biometric data with the goal of continuing to move and monitoring such movements. In fact, the platform gamifies movement by encouraging users to "collect MOVEs" (a MOVE is a unit of measurement that pertains to an individual's body and the type of move performed). MOVEs increase in number with higher rates of intensity. In the case of exercise at the YMCA, collecting MOVEs can be done somewhat automatically. Once users log in on fitness equipment, they can track and store a workout session, or they can use their smartphones to scan a QR code on the machine and track the session using their mobile phones. The mobile application readily uses the language of tracking—of MOVEs, progress, goals, and so on—to indicate the value of the platform. It offers "individualized" workouts based upon personal data streams but also suggests users "are never alone" as they can get virtual assistance that trains users to perform certain fitness plans. The user side of the app largely presents Mywellness a self-surveillance tool—that is, as a way to track and sort one's fitness patterns over a given period.

In contrast to advertisement to everyday users, Mywellness advertises its services to professional industries quite differently. On the industry-facing presence of the TechnoGym website, Mywellness is described as a platform that enables "operators to run their business more profitably by managing their clients' lifestyles" (TechnoGym 2017a). Indeed, having access to user data, gym staff and management can track clients' movements and personal information (such as weight and body-mass index). As discussed on the website, this allows the gym industry to "discover what motivates [their] members" and to "track their path to fitness with lifestyle data that's synced to their account" (TechnoGym 2017a). Here, the corporate-facing side of Mywellness directly invokes the language of surveillance. Not only can gym members be watched, but they can be tracked, monitored, and sorted—both inside the gym and outside of it—in a way that allows for maximum profits.

As discussed in both the terms of use and the privacy policy, the storing, organizing, and sharing of data are the key services on which the Mywellness platform is built. Upon signing up for the service, members must consent to sharing "sensitive data" with TechnoGym. For this platform, sensitive data include weight, body-mass index, height, gender, and age. Along with sensitive data (which, of course, may fluctuate with time), Mywellness collects, stores, and shares other forms of data related to, for example, types of exercise, frequency of exercise, and the number of calories expended in a given day. The privacy policy also indicates that information not related to fitness is gathered as well. For example, the service collects web-browsing data, data from other applications and social media platforms, and geolocation data. More than collections of data, those who sign up for Mywellness agree to share a constant stream of data—with TechnoGym, of course, but also with nondistinct "third parties" for purposes of advertising and research, with local gym staff (called "Wellness Operators" in the privacy policy), and, if applicable, with connected accounts (e.g., Apple Health, Fitbit, Garmin, Nike, etc.).

A deep-circulation view considers how the use of Mywellness and the movements generated from my body are extracted in multiple ways flowing divergently on infrastructures that grant personal-data access to many intermediaries. Access to my data will be granted to Wellness Controllers (e.g., gym staff and management) at the Y, but the data will move much farther than that. Because Mywellness is headquartered in Italy, data will travel via fiber-optic cables across transoceanic sea floors to be stored in a data center located in the European Union (Mywellness 2017). And because my data will reside in the European Union, they will get tangled up with Italian law, specifically Italian Legislative Decree no. 196, a complex legal code that designates rights for "data subjects" (those who transmit their data), as well as "data controllers" and "data processors" (the legal persons/entities that can control and process information related to data subjects). Further, if I post a status update on Facebook, I share my data with yet another platform where data flows are governed by yet another privacy and terms-of-use policy.

While it's difficult to follow the data circulations as they splinter off into myriad directions, the privacy policy for Mywellness indicates that user data may be used and trafficked for a number of reasons. These include promotional messages, market-research initiatives, and data-profiling activities. The privacy policy defines "data processing for profiling purposes" as "processing aimed at defining the profile or personality of the party concerned, or analyzing consumption habits and decisions" (Mywellness 2017). The policy indicates such profiling may be used to send users "personalized tips" about their exercise patterns and habits. Data flows from profiling move not only within the TechnoGym database but also beyond it for "advertising purposes" (Mywellness 2017). In other words, what once was a moving body on a treadmill has now been abstracted into a deep circulation, flows harnessed to build aggregated data profiles that will travel still farther to third-party intermediaries and on and on. The affective space of the Y may help energize one body—the human body—but much more will circulate beyond its bounded locale.

While it is not possible to say precisely where and how data circulate in the case of Mywellness (the purposeful obfuscation of data practices should be noted, however), there's a growing critical literature that details the abuses and exploitations inherent in the self-tracking and Quantified Self industry overall. For Lupton, self-tracking practices writ large have led to a new form of biopower in which value is derived from the human body but circulates within a digital-data economy. The result, Lupton notes, is a kind of "biocapital" that circulates within the burgeoning businesses of data harvesting and data brokering. Lupton describes many of the ways circulating data have been put to new uses by employers, insurance and credit companies, hospitals, and more. Of particular concern, these circulating

data profiles have "created new possibilities for social and economic discrimination," which can "affect people's access to
healthcare, credit, insurance, social security, educational institutions, and employment options and render them vulnerable
to unfair targeting by policing and security agencies" (2016,
85). In an age of self-tracking, circulating a life log of one's
daily exercise routines—or lack thereof—generates a kind of
vulnerability, as the biocapital extracted from such (non)move-
ments can have profound social and economic repercussions
on one's life.

Consequently, a larger cultural issue is at stake when considering the surveillance of deep circulations in the fitness-
tracking industry. It presents bodies as ready—and willing—to
be surveilled in the name of a generalized wellness and a
techno-optimist future to come. This somewhat monolithic
vision of wellness can fold back on itself to count certain bodies
and ignore or disregard others. That is, data aggregated from
fitness tracking can generate—with meticulous precision—the
metrics of the ideal body. Consider the assumptions about
the ideal users of the Mywellnness platform—their bodies are
assumed to be highly mobile, assumed to desire self-tracking,
and assumed to have a certain level of functional literacy and
leisure time. But, of course, such assumptions fail to capture
everyone's lived experiences and realities.

To rephrase an aforementioned statement: (some) bodies
move, (some) bodies keep count. What happens to those who
don't or can't? As Christa Teston argues about larger mobile-
health discourses, collecting data on movement and mobility reproduces precarious rhetorics in which some bodies are
deemed worthwhile and others are expendable. For Teston,
"Precarity gestures at how material and corporeal recognition
happens only when one submits oneself to social norms, and
how those social norms thereby condition the very way one
may be recognized" (2016, 285). Such precarious conditions of
wellness are constitutive of many health and fitness platforms
(Mywellness Cloud included): they present a method of achieving "wellness," but in order to approach any kind of benefit

from that method, a person must forgo any semblance of privacy and submit their data to flow promiscuously in opaque backstage infrastructures. Being attuned to deep circulation can help reveal a deep vulnerability that can (re)produce social inequalities as circulations fracture into various dimensionalities and become objects of surveillance and social sorting.

This case example is just one mundane space, one everyday technology in which deep circulation plays out. It is meant to show the entanglement of affective, textual, and infrastructural dimensionalities of circulation—and to demonstrate how procedures of surveillance can impinge upon or intercept each dimensionality of circulatory flow. Mywellness and the YMCA are not unique in this regard. The logics of deep circulation undergird many other writing practices other scholars in this volume investigate, including for example, posting social media, uploading material to learning-management systems, and playing casual games on mobile devices.

DEEP CIRCULATION | DEEP CITIZENSHIP

Scholars have investigated the significance of circulation for rhetorical theory, practice, and pedagogy. In particular, this work has largely paid attention to textual circulation, developing complex and innovative procedures for theorizing and researching how texts move, transform, and effect change as they circulate. What may get obscured or downplayed in such considerations, however, is what else travels with textual circulations. This chapter argues that deep circulation—with attention to affective, textual, and infrastructural circulations—provides a framework for grasping at that "else." To consider deep circulation, especially in an age of hypersurveillance, is not just a thought exercise. It offers a political and ethical lens to contemplate complexities of circulation.

Many writing practices in classrooms and beyond (e.g., designing spreadable media projects, distributing videos on YouTube, posting responses to blogs, etc.) involve more than one dimensionality of circulation. To discuss textual circulation alone, for example, may ignore the affective atmospheres that help normalize and encourage conditions of surveillance. Likewise, discrete attention to textual circulation may cast aside issues related to data circulation, for as Judith Gregory and Geoffrey Bowker argue, "The question with data is not whether data are essential, will circulate, will be used—but how so" (2016, 214). A more capacious understanding of circulation may intensify modes of analysis and open up paths for rhetorical invention.

Ultimately, the point is not to fear deep circulation but to generate new ethical and political stances for understanding, acting with, and resisting the conditions of surveillance that underpin deep flows of circulation. In other words, with deep circulation comes the need for deep citizenship. Practices of deep citizenship—very much in process and in need of more elaboration, research, and activism—can be accomplished on a number of fronts. In the context of this chapter, deep citizenship may take place at the level of everyday political practices, at the level of policy, at the level of platform design and terms of service, and, as this collection shows, at the level of educating ourselves and others about the risks of not paying attention to how information about our lives and bodies travels.

REFERENCES

Ahmed, Sara. 2004. *The Cultural Politics of Emotion.* New York: Routledge.

Amidon, Timothy, and Jessica Reyman. 2014. "Authorship and Ownership of User Contributions on the Social Web." In *Cultures of Copyright,* edited by Dànielle Nicole DeVoss and Martine Courant Rife, 108–24. New York: Peter Lang.

Bauman, Zygmunt, and David Lyon. 2013. *Liquid Surveillance: A Conversation.* Malden, MA: Polity.

Beck, Estee N. 2015. "The Invisible Digital Identity: Assemblages in Digital Networks." *Computers and Composition* 35: 125–40.

Beck, Estee N., Angela Crow, Heidi A. McKee, Colleen A. Reilly, Stephanie Vie, Laura Gonzales, and Dànielle Nicole DeVoss. 2016. "Writing in an Age of Surveillance, Privacy, and Net Neutrality." *Kairos: A Journal of Rhetoric, Technology, and Pedagogy* 20 (2): http://kairos.technorhetoric.net/20.2/topoi/beck-et-al/beck.html.

Brown, James Jr. 2015. *Ethical Programs: Hospitality and the Rhetorics of Software.* Ann Arbor: University of Michigan Press.

Chaput, Catherine. 2010. "Rhetorical Circulation in Late Capitalism: Neo-liberalism and the Overdetermination of Affective Energy." *Philosophy and Rhetoric* 43 (1): 1–25.

"deep, adj." 2020. *OED Online.* Oxford University Press. Accessed 17 September 2020. www.oed.com/view/Entry/48625.

DeVoss, Dànielle Nicole, Ellen Cushman, and Jeffrey T. Grabill. 2005. "Infrastructure and Composing: The When of New-Media Writing." *College Composition and Communication* 57 (1): 14–44.

Edbauer, Jenny. 2005. "Unframing Models of Public Distribution: From Rhetorical Situation to Rhetorical Ecologies." *Rhetoric Society Quarterly* 35 (4): 5–24.

Edwards, Dustin. 2017. "On Circulatory Encounters: The Case for Tactical Rhetorics." *Enculturation: A Journal of Rhetoric, Writing, and Culture* 25. http://enculturation.net/circulatory_encounters.

Edwards, Dustin, and Heather Lang. 2018. "Entanglements That Matter: A New Materialist Trace of #YesAllWomen." In *Circulation, Rhetoric, and Writing*, edited by Laurie Gries and Collin Brooke. Logan: Utah State University Press.

Gregory, Judith, and Geoffrey Bowker. 2016. "The Data Citizen, the Quantified Self, and Personal Genomics." In *Quantified: Biosensing Technologies in Everyday Life*, edited by Dawn Nafus, 211–24. Cambridge: MIT Press.

Gries, Laurie. 2013. "Iconographic Tracking: A Digital Research Method for Visual Rhetoric and Circulation Studies." *Computers and Composition* 30 (4): 332–48.

Gries, Laurie. 2015. *Still Life with Rhetoric: A New Materialist Approach for Visual Rhetorics.* Logan: Utah State University Press.

Haggerty, Kevin D., and Richard V. Ericson. 2000. "The Surveillant Assemblage." *British Journal of Sociology* 51 (4): 605–22.

Hawk, Byron. 2012. "Circulating Ecologies, Circulating Musics: From the Public Sphere to Sphere Publics." In *Ecology, Writing Theory, and New Media: Writing Ecology*, edited by Sidney Dobrin. New York: Routledge.

Lupton, Deborah. 2016. *The Quantified Self.* Malden, MA: Polity.

Lyon, David. 2015. *Surveillance after Snowden.* Malden, MA: Polity.

Mailloux, Steven. 2002. "Re-Marking Slave Bodies: Rhetoric as Production and Reception." *Philosophy and Rhetoric* 35 (2): 96–119.

McCormack, Derek. 2014. *Refrains for Moving Bodies: Experience and Experiment in Affective Spaces.* Durham, NC: Duke University Press.

McKee, Heidi. 2011. "Policy Matters Now and in the Future: Net Neutrality, Corporate Data Mining, and Government Surveillance." *Computers and Composition* 28 (4): 276–91.

McNely, Brian. 2016. "Circulatory Intensities: Take a Book | Leave a Book." In *Rhetoric, Through Everyday Things*, edited by Scot Barnett and Casey Boyle. Tuscaloosa: University of Alabama Press.

Mywellness. 2017. "Privacy Policy." Accessed in 2017. https://6560a8ab83e11d3 1e5b8a6a2f3b6d8cd41e62196a5824547b1d8.ssl.cf3.rackcdn.com/privacy /en-us/privacy.html.

Neff, Gina, and Dawn Nafus. 2016. *Self-Tracking.* Cambridge: MIT Press.

Parikka, Jussi. 2015. *A Geology of Media*. Minneapolis: University of Minnesota Press.

Parks, Lisa, and Nicole Starosielski. 2015. Introduction to *Signal Traffic: Critical Studies of Media Infrastructures*, edited by Lisa Parks and Nicole Starosielski, 1–30. Urbana: University of Illinois Press.

Pasquale, Frank. 2015. *The Black Box Society: The Secret Algorithms That Control Money and Information*. Cambridge, MA: Harvard University Press.

Reyman, Jessica. 2013. "User Data on the Social Web: Authorship, Agency, and Appropriation." *College English* 75 (5): 513–33.

Ridolfo, Jim. 2015. *Digital Samaritans: Rhetorical Delivery and Engagement in the Digital Humanities*. Ann Arbor: University of Michigan Press.

Ridolfo, Jim, and Dànielle Nicole DeVoss. 2009. "Composing for Recomposition: Rhetorical Velocity and Delivery." *Kairos: A Journal of Rhetoric, Technology, and Pedagogy* 13 (2). http://kairos.technorhetoric.net/13.2/topoi/ridolfo_devoss/intro.html.

Seigworth, Gregory J., and Melissa Gregg. 2010. "An Inventory of Shimmers." In *The Affect Theory Reader*, edited by Gregory Seigworth and Melissa Gregg, 1–25. Durham, NC: Duke University Press.

Stewart, Kathleen. 2011. "Atmospheric Attunements." *Environment and Planning D: Society and Space* 29 (3): 445–53.

TechnoGym. 2017a. "Business Solution." https://www.technogym.com/us/business-solution/mywellness-2/.

TechnoGym. 2017b. "Who We Are." http://www.technogym.com/us/who-we-are/facts-and-figures/.

Teston, Christa. 2016. "Rhetoric, Precarity, and mHealth Technologies." *Rhetoric Society Quarterly* 46 (3): 251–61.

Trimbur, John. 2000. "Composition and the Circulation of Writing." *College Composition and Communication* 52 (2): 188–219.

van der Ploeg, Irma. 2012. "The Body as Data in the Age of Information." In *Routledge Handbook of Surveillance Studies*, edited by Kirstie Ball, Kevin Haggerty, and David Lyon, 176–84. New York: Routledge.

Warner, Michael. 2005. *Publics and Counterpublics*. New York: Zone Books.

5

DIGITAL LITERACY IN AN AGE OF PERVASIVE SURVEILLANCE
A Case of Wearable Technology

Jason Tham and Ann Hill Duin

Advances in computer technologies have created *big data*: extremely large data sets that are analyzed computationally to infer, predict, and locate patterns relating to human behavior. Big data's focus is statistical; accuracy increases as its data sets grow larger. Because each of us "leaves a trail of digital exhaust, an infinite stream of phone records, texts, browser histories, GPS [global positioning system] data, and other information that will live on forever," (Smolan and Erwitt 2012, 9), data sets grow exponentially. The analysis of such big data can detect our personal and learning behavior patterns, many of which we are not aware, which can then be used for targeted marketing, as well as targeted teaching and learning strategies. Evidently, big data can be very useful to higher education, as experts contend (Else 2017). How those of us in higher education obtain, use, and disseminate these data, however, remains debatable.

From social networking and gaming apps to health and wellness trackers, to new communicative features like emojis and animojis, to online collaborative tools such as Google Docs, we compose in virtual spaces where the contents of our communication can be easily duplicated, shared, and made public with or without our permission. Our field has long engaged in debates and discussions about the rhetorics surrounding these technologies, particularly privacy, information security, and student writing in composition pedagogy (Beck 2015, 2016; Hawisher and Selfe 1991; Purdy 2009; Reyman 2013). As we continue to

DOI: 10.7330/9781646420315.c005

scrutinize the impact of new digital environments on our work, this chapter highlights the need to expand on current conceptions of digital literacies to encompass the evolving issues of privacy, surveillance, and pervasive computing. Our goal is to attend to how recent developments in academic data collection challenge our understanding of information ownership and agency. We do so by looking at a case of pervasive data collection through a wearable technology.

The top concern related to the use of wearables in education is privacy (Bower and Sturman 2015). Since many higher education institutions are beginning to experiment with embodied technologies and ubiquitous data collection (e.g., Coalition for Networked Information 2016; Dede, Ho, and Mitros 2016), universities could face potential privacy and security complaints or even lawsuits if they slip up when implementing their wearable technology programs. For rhetoric and composition scholars, the issue with ubiquitous data mining in the academy does not end at the legal level; it must be expanded to include discussions of surveillance and self-tracking and how they impact our acts of composing. Joining the voices of those in this collection, such as Gavin P. Johnson's and his critique of grading technologies operating as surveillance, we offer a critique of the Fitbit integration program at Oral Roberts University, a private evangelical liberal arts university in Tulsa, Oklahoma. The exigence we see through this case study is the increasing complexity of adopting data analytics in the academy and the need for faculty members and students to participate in the data collection and analysis processes—not leaving those processes solely in the hands of administrators and data analytics companies. In the end, we would like our readers to ask questions regarding their use of digital technologies and how they situate themselves in the larger context of pervasive surveillance.

LITERATURE REVIEW

Unsurprisingly, privacy risks grow as systems and devices become more connected. In a May 2014 report from the Executive

Office of the President of the United States, the Obama administration acknowledges the critical issues revolving around data personalization, data deidentification and reidentification, and data-storage practices. These issues present formidable challenges to wearable technology. In his editorial introduction in the journal *IEEE Internet Computing*, Drexel University provost M. Brian Blake writes that wearables can provide significant service to individuals and institutions alike given their connectivity to databases and augmented physical monitoring. However, researchers and administrators should pay attention to several areas concerning the privacy and cybersecurity of wearers:

- *Safe collaboration*: Collaborating among users while preserving privacy of individuals, including biological and location-based information.
- *Ethical use*: Instilling moral protocol to wearable devices' operations that prevent misuse.
- *Data accuracy*: Leveraging on collective intelligence, or big data, while preventing intentional or malicious tampering of information. (2015, 4–5)

Given the emphasis on activity and health-related monitoring by wearable devices, wearers might be exposed to the risk of discrimination related to genetics information, medical records, and personal identities, as such information is quantified by embodied sensors and trackers. Two areas for concern are how the mandated integration of wearable devices invades individual rights to privacy and how the data generated from the integration program might be used beyond educational intentions.

Privacy, according to the *Human Subject Institutional Review Board (IRB) Guidebook*, published by the Office for Human Research Protections (OHRP), "can be defined in terms of having control over the extent, timing, and circumstances of sharing oneself (physically, behaviorally, or intellectually) with others" (2013). Social scientists and humanities researchers who have undergone the basic IRB investigator training modules are taught this compliance definition of privacy, with little variation, depending on the training program their institutions employ: "privacy refers to the right to control access to ourselves and to our personal information. Privacy means we have the right to control the degree, the timing, and the conditions for sharing our bodies, thoughts, and experiences with others. Privacy must be protected before and during the recruitment of subjects, the consent process, and participation in the research activity. Methods to protect subject privacy include conducting research activities in a private setting or ensuring that data are not collected without the individual's knowledge and consent" (Collaborative Institutional Training Initiative 2012).

Whether it is the IRB research compliance definition of privacy, or the federal versions that protect student personal information, such as the Family Educational Rights and Privacy Act (FERPA), these definitions are legally bound on a technical level. But privacy is more than just technical; privacy is often a sensed notion and is "socially contingent, more socially constructed, and more culturally relative than other rights" (Schauer 2001, 221). Andreas Kotsios writes in Oxford's *International Journal of Law and Information Technology* that "legal conceptualization of privacy is very difficult" (2015, 165). Citing law professor Stephen Henderson, Kotsios highlights the contested notion of privacy—that "almost everyone agrees that we should have it, but has different ideas of just what it is" (2012, 232). Legal scholars have tried to organize the multilayer privacy concept into taxonomies related to information collection, information processing, information dissemination, and invasion (Kotsios 2015; Solove 2008). Recent developments on new technologies and their uses continue to expand the legal taxonomies of privacy to include socioeconomic and political aspects, such as freedom of speech, choice of sexual preference and religion, and the overall strengthening of democracy (Finn, Wright, and Friedewald 2013). For program administrators, these typologies are useful starting points to consider how students' privacy can be protected if they are required to use wearable devices for educational purposes.

When compiled and analyzed, wearable-device data can reveal much personal information about students. Although student wearers might have the option to choose what information to disclose—such as location, heart rate, and activity summary—many do not fully understand the types and volume of information being gathered about them or the implications of sharing that information (Karanasiou and Kang 2016). Studies on user perception of wearable data collection show a high prevalence of an implicit sense of user control and that users are not usually aware of security and privacy threats against their monitoring devices (Bellekens et al. 2016). We see this as a literacy issue.

The social dimension of issues concerning privacy is as complicated as the legal and technological. Sociotechnical discussions of the intersections of identity and technology are continually confronted with tensions among technological affordances, user experience, and user expressions of identities. While wearables are increasingly used as identity-management tools—that is, devices that allow users to manage their digital profiles across various platforms—they can at the same time define, expose, or modify the identities of their users. In "Mapping the Margins," Kimberlé Crenshaw argues that "identity categories" such as race, color, and sexual orientation "are most often treated in mainstream liberal discourse as vestiges of bias or domination" (1993, 1242). For scholars of rhetoric and writing, this aspect of identity and privacy in an age of pervasive media is thus more than just a legal concern. We must pay attention to how intersectional identities are affected by pervasive surveillance technologies.

A CASE OF WEARABLE TECHNOLOGY

Whether they are smartwatches, fitness bracelets, optical head-mounted displays, or badges individuals wear to capture their interactions with others in personal or professional settings, wearable technologies are becoming fashionable across private and public sectors. In a recent study, Matt Bower and Daniel Sturman (2015) question the educational affordances of wearable technologies and find that gathering in situ contextual information, recording, and simulation capabilities emerged as top pedagogical uses for these technologies. Outside the

classroom, wearable devices also provide wireless connectivity, real-time activity analytics, and unobtrusive interfaces that
alert the wearer to complete certain tasks. To date, a handful of
higher education institutions have launched campus-wide wearable programs as part of their student-engagement strategies
(Mathewson 2017). At Oral Roberts University (ORU), incoming freshmen in fall 2015 were asked to use Fitbit, a wrist-worn
fitness tracker, to monitor their physical activity and earn aerobics points for the university's physical-fitness requirements.

For the purpose of context, ORU is a faith-based university.
It values a "Christian worldview" and has an honor code[1] all its
constituents abide by, including faculty members and students:
"Every professor and student on the ORU campus shares a
Christian worldview and a dedication to a common purpose.
Our campus is spiritually alive. Class opens with prayer. We
gather twice weekly for chapel and opportunities for student-
led worship and service abound" (Oral Roberts, "Christian
Worldview," n.d.). We kept this honor code in mind when analyzing the Fitbit integration program, as it informs how the university views certain ideologies and its definition of ethics and
acceptable behaviors.

In many press interviews, ORU president William M. Wilson
has been quoted extolling the "unique educational approaches"
his university offers through "the marriage of new technology"
with the existing physical-activity requirements for students
(Allen 2016). The university distinguishes itself by focusing on
the "whole person"—mind, body, and spirit—and not just the
academic achievements of its students. According to ORU's
website, the whole-person assessment program was introduced
in 2002 "as a means for students and their professors to measure a student's progress toward goals while at ORU. . . . It has
become the primary data-gathering instrument for personal
assessment" (Oral Roberts, "Whole Person Assessment," n.d.).
Under one of the five student learning outcomes, students
are expected to be "physically disciplined" by achieving the
proficiencies and capacities of a "healthy lifestyle" and "physically disciplined lifestyle." To demonstrate these achievements,

students earn "aerobic points" that count toward these proficiency areas.

In spring 2009, ORU enhanced the promotion of the whole-person curriculum by rewarding "Quest Whole Person Scholarships" to students who "exemplify the whole person lifestyle" (Oral Roberts, "Quest Whole Person Scholarship," n.d.). As displayed prominently on the scholarship website, students who demonstrate "wholeness" in "Christian Worldview, Lifestyle of Service, Academic Achievement, Leadership Ability, Vision to Make a Life-Changing Impact on Others, and a Healthy Lifestyle" are considered for a renewable $20,000 annual scholarship. While it is offered only to incoming freshmen or transfer students, students who would like to renew their application for the scholarship are required to maintain wholeness in the said criteria. This, combined with the whole-person assessment program, makes a justificatory argument for Fitbit integration at ORU.

Prior to the fitness-trackers integration, ORU students simply had to keep a fitness journal and log aerobic points manually. With the Fitbit integration, students can let their trackers feed aerobics points automatically to the gradebook on their learning-management system, Brightspace by Desire2Learn. Although students can choose between adopting the Fitbit pilot program or logging their activity manually, the ORU president has stated that "those who choose to utilize Fitbits will reap the benefits of a more convenient fitness tracking system" (Oral Roberts, "Oral Roberts University Integrates," 2016).

Expectedly, the ORU Fitbit-integration program was received with more disapproval than favor from the public. Backlash began brewing just two months into the start of the pilot program. On Twitter, the hashtag "#DontTrackMe" trended and was said to have originated from the National Eating Disorders Association and its body-positive platform, Proud2BMe. On February 22, 2016, writer Kaitlin Irwin's post on the *National Eating Disorders Association Blog* slammed the ORU fitness-tracking mandate and urged readers to sign a petition requesting that the university remove the program from student

graduation requirements. Besides the concern for misunder-
standings about what "healthy lifestyle" means, Irwin and those
against tracking student activities using Fitbit were enraged that
students were going to be constantly under the surveillance of
the university should they wear their Fitbit trackers all the time.
The Daily Beast writer Samantha Allen pointed out, "ORU has
set a goal of 10,000 steps per day for participants in the freshman program. For most new freshmen walkers, that will come
out to around 5 miles a day. None of those steps, mind you,
should be used to walk hand-in-hand with someone of the same
sex, as the school's honor code requires complete abstinence
from 'any homosexual activity.' Nor should they be taken after
1:30 a.m., which is the curfew for all students living on ORU
campus, or while wearing clothing that violates the school's
extensive dress code" (2016). Allen's angst addressed only a
few of the many arguments that arise when it comes to tracking
and surveillance. It is particularly interesting when such arguments are placed in the context of the university's honor code
and faith values. How might the Fitbit trackers serve as a surveillance tool besides providing activity data to the faculty? To what
extent are ethics and privacy intertwining?

Among the fiercest arguments against the integration of
Fitbit at ORU was one arising from the fear of identity oppression. As Allen asserts, those who petitioned to stop tracking
student activity for fitness points were worried that their activity data might expose layers of identity some students might
prefer to keep private from their school administration and
faculty members. Such fear is not without reason; the potential
and real discrimination against particular identity expressions
due to the quantification and exposure of student activity can
pose serious threats to the integrity of education. For instance,
students whose physical-activity data do not reflect the typical
or required (ten thousand steps) performance—which may be
achievable only by those who are able-bodied—might be seen
as less engaged or motivated by the "healthy lifestyle" defined
by the university and its honor code. These data might generate a certain image for underperforming students, giving them

a potentially undesirable label that privileges only those who are able to meet the standards. For these students, their under-performance (in the eyes of the university) might lead to peer pressure, self-doubt, and unnecessary anxiety.

Combined with the lack of critical awareness around the collection, aggregation, and sharing of personal data, plus the absence of what Blake (2015) calls a moral protocol[2] for the use of this data, a seemingly invasive technological integra-tion such as the ORU Fitbit program would only engender negative responses. In the ORU case, we observe little faculty involvement in such decision-making (as seen in reports of the program, such as Asseo et al. 2016 and Sherman, *Tulsa World,* January 17, 2016), especially those whose research could inform this kind of radical implementation. Acknowledging the prolif-eration of wearables, we argue, scholars in writing studies can challenge the popular assumptions of surveillance and privacy. Our disciplinary research positions us well to scrutinize what it means to watch and be watched, to question what counts as personal and analyze what counts as public in the face of per-vasive or ubiquitous computing, and to and identify who owns big data so we can teach critical use of emerging technologies (Duin et al. 2016). We enter this discussion from the perspec-tive of digital literacy.

DISCUSSION
Expanding Digital Literacy: Data Literacy and Participatory Design

The rise of new media and digital technologies continues to capture the attention of literacy scholars. Due to the affor-dances of pervasive data collection by these ubiquitous tech-nologies, scholars have been studying the politics of these new interfaces in our literate lives, including ideological perspec-tives (Palmquist 2006; Selfe and Hawisher 2006; Selfe and Selfe 1994), access and intellectual property (Fisher et al. 2006; Logie 1998), and surveillance issues (see Beck and Hutchinson Campos's introduction to this collection). All these stud-ies emphasize the need for students and teachers to acquire awareness and skills to navigate the new technological terrains. In the case of wearable technologies and learning analytics, scholars have shown concern regarding the potential invasion of these technologies into teaching and learning (Bower and Stuman 2015). The two of us argue that, in an age of pervasive surveillance, writing studies scholars must pay attention to digital literacy.

Two decades ago, Paul Gilster (1997) introduced us to the concept of digital literacy, arguing that the most needed literate ability in digital environments is making educated judgments when finding, verifying, and incorporating online content into one's work. Extending the works of Gilster to our field, Cynthia Selfe urged composition and writing studies scholars to pay attention to computer technology and its links to literacy education (1999). Selfe argued that literacy instructors, including English and writing scholars, have the professional responsibility to understand the ways digital technology affects how students learn and lead their lives. Echoing Selfe, Laura Gurak, in *Cyberliteracy: Navigating the Internet with Awareness*, asserts that digital literacy is "not simply a matter of learning how to keep up with the technology or how to do a Web search. For communication technologies shape our social and cultural spaces" (2001, 27). To "become aware of technology," Gurak argues, "should be to become curious" (27) and "an active participant in the discussion," that is, "to become better at critiquing, challenging, and anticipating how these technologies are designed, implemented, and used" (28).

The writing and technical communication community has since responded to both Selfe's and Gurak's calls by continually exploring the complex links among technology, literacy, and culture. Lee-Ann Kastman Breuch, in capturing the effects of technology on our reading and writing practices, coined "technological literacy" to describe "scholarship that addresses the ability to use technology; the ability to read, write, and communicate using technology; and the ability to think critically about technology" (2002, 269). In *Digital Literacy for Technical Communication: 21st Century Theory and Practice*, Rachel Spilka defines digital literacy as not just "the ability to read, write, and communicate using digital technology" but also "the ability to think critically about digital technology, and consideration of social, cultural, political, and educational values associated with those activities" (2010, 8). Scholars like Spilka, Breuch, Gurak, and Selfe advance a critical approach to technology consumption and production. To that end, Stephanie Vie emphasizes the need for instructors to "examine the complexities" of new media such as social networking sites and the ramifications they have on our pedagogy (2008, 23).

In the face of pervasive computing and data mining, however, a critical awareness of digital literacy that focuses on the cultural, political, and other social aspects of technology must be supplemented by a contextual consideration of agency. In the case of wearable technologies and academic analytics, we recommend that users rethink what they consider to be private and public and recognize the rhetorical contexts wherein their privacy and identities must be negotiated. For instance, in ORU's Fitbit integration, there should be critical conversations about the intent of such technological integration among students, faculty members, and the public. As users who are directly impacted by this program, students must understand the rhetorical context in which they see their place and purpose in the Fitbit program. On this, we find Jenni Swenson's (2015) heuristics to be especially helpful. We provide a list of recommendations in the following section; however, at this point, we suggest the following questions for students to ask who are participating in an analytics program similar to ORU's Fitbit integration program:

- What data are being collected?
- Who has access to these data?
- What control do I have over these data?
- How are these data being analyzed and used? How might they affect me?
- What can I do to participate in the data analytics program/process?

Using these questions as a guide, faculty members can work with students to discuss how their personal information reveals fragments of their identities to instructors and the institution. In these conversations, students and faculty members can negotiate how best to use the aggregated data in an educational context. This approach gives students the agency to participate knowing they are not just subjects but contributors to a program.

Critical digital literacy should also emphasize data literacy. In an age when platforms quantify and extrapolate user data for trends—whether in marketing, politics, or learning—we must add to our curriculum an ongoing cultivation of data literacy to support students and instructors working to understand how to read, create, and communicate data as information. Laurie Gries defines data literacy as the ability to "gather, evaluate, visualize, draw conclusions from, and communicate data to form new knowledge" (2017). As other chapters in this collection show, data literacy can be integrated into our writing programs so students can learn to examine the data-conceptualization, collection, analysis, and presentation process. To respond to potential arguments about the place of data literacy in composition and writing studies, we contend that writing is data generation and communication, and written communication is becoming intertwined with digital information constituted by accessible data. Thus, students need to acquire the necessary skills to understand what data mean and how to draw inferences from data sets. A critical data-literacy process would teach students to see "how data are applied for benefit or detriment, within the cultural context of security and privacy" (Crusoe 2016, 38).

Most importantly, we argue that it is crucial for institutions to employ a participatory approach to designing and instating their pervasive data-collection infrastructures. Of course, participation among faculty, staff, and students does not naturally lead to less resistance to pervasive data collection. However, participation creates a forum for those who are affected by the analytics program to voice their concerns and recommendations, and it allows the potential for their voices to be heard. From the perspective of social constructivism, participation also allows for collocation of expertise and justificatory arguments concerning the design of data analytics programs. Such a participatory approach is not only ethical but also "value-driven" (Bergold and Thomas 2012).

User participation is imperative to the success of learning-technologies integration. One thing we have learned is that participation of stakeholders and subjects is needed for high-stakes processes such as the implementation of a new monitoring system or transitioning to a new platform that would impact the way users work on a daily basis. By planning and conducting the change process with those whose lifeworld and meaningful actions are under study, "The participatory research process enables co-researchers to step back cognitively from familiar routines, forms of interaction, and power relationships in order to fundamentally question and rethink established interpretations of situations and strategies" (Bergold and Thomas 2012). We include this approach as part of the expansion of digital literacy, as it compels us to always consider collaboration rather than isolation when dealing with digital tools, especially when the process concerns issues of privacy, sharing, and security.

Implications for Writing Infrastructures: Some Ethical Heuristics

The primary focus of this edited collection is the impact of surveillance on our human acts of composing—within and outside the classroom. The ORU case represents a wake-up call regarding pervasive surveillance by technologies deployed by higher-ed institutions. Among lessons learned from this case study is the fact that we do not know where our data goes or how they will be used when students wear Fitbits. According to Francisco de Arriba-Perez, Manuel Caeiro-Rodriguez, and Juan Manuel Santos-Gago, "Data from Fitbit quantification bands . . . enables third-party developers to get such data through the REST API" (2016, 7). The impact of surveillance on learning will increase exponentially. Our goal is to create this critical awareness about data practices. Writing program administrators must take into account how students as individuals and their texts are quantified by readily available learning tools for multiple purposes at the university. We do our programs a disservice if we choose to ignore or discount the effort of big data analytics in the academy. What we must be concerned about is the ethical dimension of such analytical work.

Earlier we note Swenson's research on learning analytics. From summarizing and combining four existing frameworks—Mark Ward's questions regarding ethical behavior (2010); Heather Canary's teaching with ethical actions (2007); Aristotle's ethical characteristics of goodwill, practical skills, and practical wisdom (ethos); and Stuart Selber's multiliteracies (rhetorical, critical, functional) (2004)—Swenson built a set of matrices that include strategies and choices for responding in a participatory way to concerns in learning analytics. Included in the matrix regarding the application of learning analytics are the following "functional literacy" recommendations that most closely relate to students and instructors:

- Employ data designers to guide the design of visualizations and dashboards with the goal of providing context to data, elevating students over data rather than viewing students as data; of raising awareness of the rhetorical aspects of learning analytics; and of the ethical concerns related to the discriminatory aspects of learning analytics (bias, labeling, profiling)
- Provide an opt-in that includes a "release from harm" [statement] using transparent language to describe data capture, predictive modeling variables, and probability of inaccuracies
- Provide students with an opportunity to update their data records through direct feedback in order to provide context and/or explain why their label does not reflect their academic performance (give students a voice)
- Use informed consent to obtain permission for data and be transparent with all instances of data manipulation
- Create institutional best practices for using learning analytics and train faculty and staff on best practices
- Provide data privacy training to faculty and staff and minimize access to private student data to "need to know" personnel. (2015, 111–12)

These ethical recommendations are useful heuristics for evaluating our existing programs and charting future writing infrastructures—especially with regard to wearable technologies and data collection on students. Note in these recommendations the importance of allowing faculty and student engagement with the data analytics process while protecting student privacy.

Writing studies scholars and instructors can play a role in designing innovative technological integration like wearable technologies that serves the pedagogical objectives of the institution while still advocating for students' right to agency. Given our field's expertise in seeing rhetorical agency through critiques and empirical studies, as well as the emerging movement around making and building (see Sheridan 2010; Shipka 2011), we can create pathways to intervene in student data analytics programs. Some of these pathways might lead us to committees or university governance positions where we advocate for students; other roads might require us to take on the responsibility of inventing tools that protect student data while assessing their work.

CONCLUSION

In this chapter, we work to highlight the increasingly blurry line between personal and public data collected through wearable technology, problematizing the ownership of big data in higher education settings. Our acts of "wearing" and "composing" are not neutral. ORU students are expected to be "physically disciplined" by achieving the proficiencies and capacities of a "healthy lifestyle" and "physically disciplined lifestyle." To demonstrate these achievements, students earn "aerobic points" that count toward these proficiency areas. The increasing capture of academic and learning analytics identifies students who are achieving the proficiencies and competencies associated with student composing outcomes and assignments.

Our goal in this chapter is to create critical awareness about digital literacy and wearable integration in an age of pervasive surveillance. We know we have merely touched the surface on this important topic. Further investigations must be conducted to expand our field's understanding of academic analytics and associated technologies. To help frame future conversations on academic big data, surveillance, and digital literacy, we close with the following guiding questions:

- How might writing scholars and instructors participate in the shaping of future programs and related policies on academic data collection?
- How might we best make transparent to instructors and students the many contexts within which data is collected and used? How might we problematize data ownership and work to build informed data generators?

As we aim to demonstrate in this chapter, integrating pervasive data-collecting technologies in the academy doesn't necessarily address the issues of data security and individual vulnerabilities. We must create legal, technological, and social frameworks that address these issues. As writing researchers, instructors, and program administrators, we all must engage in this conversation.

ACKNOWLEDGMENTS

We thank members of the Emerging Technologies Research Collaboratory (http://etrc.umn.edu) for inspiration on this project and their ideas on integrating emerging technologies in writing pedagogy. We also thank the editors of this collection for their advice and direction during the development of this chapter.

NOTES

1. See ORU's Code of Honor Pledge here: http://www.oru.edu/pdfs/honor-code/HonorCode-2016.pdf.
2. A moral protocol involves developing organic procedures for wearable devices' operations that prevent misuse.

REFERENCES

Allen, Samantha. 2016. "The College with Mandatory Fitness Tracking Devices." *Daily Beast*, January 11. http://www.thedailybeast.com/articles/2016/01/11/the-college-with-mandatory-fitness-tracking-devices.html.

Asseo, Itai, Maggie Johnson, Bob Nilsson, Chalapathy Neti, and T. J. Costello. 2016. "The Internet of Things: Riding the Wave in Higher Education." *Educause Review*, (July/August): 11–31. https://er.educause.edu/~/media/files/articles/2016/6/erm1641.pdf.

Beck, Estee N. 2015. "The Invisible Digital Identity: Assemblages of Digital Networks." *Computers and Composition* 35: 125–40. http://dx.doi.org/10.1016/j.compcom.2015.01.005.

Beck, Estee N. 2016. "Writing Educator Responsibilities for Discussing the History and Practice of Surveillance and Privacy in Writing Classrooms." *Kairos: A Journal of Rhetoric, Technology, and Pedagogy* 20 (2). http://technorhetoric.net/20.2/topoi/beck-et-al/beck.html.

Bellekens, Xavier, Kamila Nierodzinski, Alexandra Bellekens, Preetila Seeam, Andrew Hamilton, and Amar Seeam. 2016. "A Study on Situational Awareness Security and Privacy of Wearable Health Monitoring Devices." *International Journal on Cyber Situational Awareness* 1 (1): 74–96. http://www.c-mric.org/ijcsa/article4.pdf.

Bergold, Jarg, and Stefan Thomas. 2012. "Participatory Research Methods: A Methodological Approach in Motion." *Forum: Qualitative Social Research* 13 (1): http://www.qualitative-research.net/index.php/fqs/article/view/1801/3334.

Blake, M. Brian. 2015. "Worry about Wearables." *IEEE Internet Computing* 19 (5): 4–5.

Bower, Matt, and Daniel Sturman. 2015. "What Are the Educational Affordances of Wearable Technologies?" *Computers & Education* 88: 343–53.

Breuch, Lee-Ann Kastman. 2002. "Thinking Critically about Technology Literacy: Developing a Framework to Guide Computer Pedagogy in Technical Communication." *Technical Communication Quarterly* 11 (3): 267–88.

Canary, Heather E. 2007. "Teaching Ethics in Communication Courses: An Investigation of Instructional Methods, Course Foci, and Student Outcomes." *Communication Education* 56 (2): 193–208.

Coalition for Networked Information. 2016. *Privacy in the Age of Analytics: Report of a CNI Executive Roundtable*. https://www.cni.org/wp-content/uploads/2016/08/CNI-privacy-analytics-ERreport.pdf.

Collaborative Institutional Training Initiative. 2012. "CITI Program Social/Behavioral or Humanist Research Investigators and Key Personnel." SBE Refresher 1—Privacy and Confidentiality. https://about.citiprogram.org/en/course/human-subjects-research-social-behavioral-educational-sbe-refresher-1/.

Crenshaw, Kimberlé W. 1993. "Mapping the Margins: Intersectionality, Identity Politics, and Violence against Women of Color." *Stanford Law Review* 43 (6): 1241–99.

Crusoe, David. 2016. "Data Literacy Defined Pro Populo: To Read This Article, Please Provide a Little Information." *Journal of Community Informatics* 12 (3): 27–46. http://ci-journal.org/index.php/ciej/article/view/1290.

de Arriba-Perez, Francisco, Manuel Caeiro-Rodriguez, and Juan M. Santos-Gago. 2016. "Collection and Processing of Data from Wrist Wearable Devices in Heterogeneous and Multiple-User Scenarios." *Sensors* 16 (9). doi: 10.3390/s16091538.

Dede, Chris, Andrew Ho, and Piotr Mitros. 2016. "Big Data Analysis in Higher Education: Promises and Pitfalls." *EDUCAUSE Review* 22–34. http://er.educause.edu/~/media/files/articles/2016/8/erm1652.pdf.

Duin, Ann H., Joe Moses, Megan McGrath, and Jason Tham. 2016. "Wearable Computing, Wearable Composing: New Dimensions in Composition Pedagogy." *Computers and Composition Online.* http://cconlinejournal.org/wearable/.

Else, Holly. 2017. "How Do Universities Use Big Data?" *Times Higher Education,* April 13. https://www.timeshighereducation.com/features/how-do-universities-use-big-data.

Executive Office of the President of the United States. 2014. Big Data: Seizing Opportunities, Preserving Values. May 2014. https://obamawhitehouse.archives.gov/sites/default/files/docs/big_data_privacy_report_may_1_2014.pdf.

Finn, Rachel L., David Wright, and Michael Friedewald. 2013. "Seven Types of Privacy." In *European Data Protection: Coming of Age,* edited by Serge Gutwirth, Ronald Leenes, Paul de Hert, and Yves Poullet, 3–32. New York: Springer.

Fisher, William, John Palfrey, Urs Gasser, William McGeveran, and Jackie Harlow. 2006. "The Digital Learning Challenge: Obstacles to Educational Uses of Copyrighted Material in the Digital Age." Berkman Center Research Publication No. 2006-09. https://cyber.harvard.edu/publications/2006/The_Digital_Learning_Challenge.

Gilster, Paul. 1997. *Digital Literacy.* Hoboken, NJ: John Wiley & Sons.

Gries, Laurie. 2017. "Mapping Obama Hope: A Data Visualization Project for Visual Rhetorics." *Kairos: A Journal of Rhetoric, Technology, and Pedagogy* 21 (2). http://kairos.technorhetoric.net/21.2/topoi/gries/index.html.

Gurak, Laura. 2001. *Cyberliteracy: Navigating the Internet with Awareness.* New Haven, CT: Yale University Press.

Hawisher, Gail E., and Cynthia L. Selfe. 1991. "The Rhetoric of Technology and the Electronic Writing Class." *College Composition and Communication* 42 (1): 55–65.

Henderson, Stephen E. 2012. "Expectations of Privacy in Social Media." *Mississippi College Law Review* 31: 227–47.

Karanasiou, Argyro P., and Sharanjit Kang. 2016. "My Quantified Self, My Fitbit, and I: The Polymorphic Concept of Health Data and the Sharer's Dilemma." *Digital Culture and Society* 2 (1): 123–42. https://doi.org/10.14361/dcs-2016-0109.

Kotsios, Andreas. 2015. "Privacy in an Augmented Reality." *International Journal of Law and Information Technology* 23 (2): 157–85.

Logie, John. 1998. "Champing at the Bits: Computers, Copyright, and the Composition Classroom." *Computers and Composition* 15 (2): 201–14.

Mathewson, T. G. 2017. "Fitbit for Education: Turning School into a Data-Tracking Game." Hechinger Report, November 29. http://hechingerreport.org/fitbit-education-turning-school-data-tracking-game/.

Office of Human Research Protections. 1993. *Human Subject Institutional Review Board (IRB) Guidebook.* Rockville, MD: Office of Human Research Protections.

Oral Roberts University. n.d. "Christian worldview." Accessed December 2017. http://www.oru.edu/academics/christian-worldview.php.

Oral Roberts University. n.d. "Oral Roberts University Integrates Wearable Technology with Physical Fitness Curriculum for Incoming Students." Accessed December 2017. http://www.oru.edu/news/oru_news/20160104_fitbit_tracking.php.

Oral Roberts University. "Quest Whole Person Scholarship." Accessed December 2017. http://questscholarship.org/.

Oral Roberts University. n.d. "Whole Person Assessment." Accessed December 2017. http://www.oru.edu/academics/resources/whole-person-assessment.php.

Palmquist, Mike. 2006. "Rethinking Instructional Metaphors for Web-Based Writing Environments." In *Writing and Digital Media*, edited by Luuk Van Waes, Marielle Leijten, and Christophe Neuwirth, 199–219. Oxford: Elsevier.

Purdy, James. 2009. "Anxiety and the Archive: Understanding Plagiarism Detection Services as Digital Services." *College Composition and Communication* 26 (2): 65–77.

Reyman, Jessica. 2013. "User Data on the Social Web: Authorship, Agency, and Appropriation." *College English* 75 (5): 513–33.

Schauer, Frederick. 2001. "Free Speech and the Social Construction of Privacy." *Social Research* 68 (1): 221–32.

Selber, Stuart. 2004. *Multiliteracies for a Digital Age.* Carbondale: Southern Illinois University Press.

Selfe, Cynthia L. 1999. "Technology and Literacy: A Story about the Perils of Not Paying Attention." *College Composition and Communication* 50 (3): 411–36.

Selfe, Cynthia L., and Gail E. Hawisher. 2006. "Literacies and the Complexities of the Global Digital Divide." In *Writing and Digital Media*, edited by Luuk Van Waes, Marielle Leijten, and Christophe Neuwirth, 253–85. Oxford: Elsevier.

Selfe, Cynthia L., and Richard J. Selfe. 1994. "The Politics of the Interface: Power and Its Exercise in Electronic Contact Zones." *College Composition and Communication* 45 (4): 480–504.

Sheridan, David M. 2010. "Fabricating Consent: Three-Dimensional Objects as Rhetorical Compositions." *Computers and Composition* 27 (4): 249–65.

Sherman, Bill. 2016. "ORU Freshmen Are All Wearing Fitness Trackers in Pioneer Program." *Tulsa World*, January 7. http://www.tulsaworld.com/news/religion/oru-freshmen-are-all-wearing-fitness-trackers-in-pioneer-program/article_38e95c1c-a584-5bbc-875c-910f241958e8.html.

Shipka, Jody. 2011. *Toward a Composition Made Whole.* Pittsburgh: University of Pittsburgh Press.

Smolan, Rick, and Jennifer Erwitt. 2012. *The Human Face of Big Data.* New York: Against All Odds Productions.

Solove, Daniel J. 2008. *Understanding Privacy.* Cambridge, MA: Harvard University Press.

Spilka, Rachel. 2010. *Digital Literacy for Technical Communication: 21st Century Theory and Practice*. New York: Routledge.

Swenson, Jenni. 2015. "Understanding Ethical Concerns in the Design, Application, and Documentation of Learning Analytics in Post-Secondary Education." PhD diss., University of Minnesota.

Vie, Stephanie. 2008. "Digital Divide 2.0: 'Generation M' and Online Social Networking Sites in the Composition Classroom." *Computers and Composition* 25 (1): 9–23.

Ward, Mark Sr. 2010. "The Ethics of Exigence: Information Design, Postmodern Ethics, and the Holocaust." *Journal of Business and Technical Communication* 24 (1): 60–90.

6

GOTTA WATCH 'EM ALL
Privacy, Social Gameplay, and Writing in Augmented Reality Games

Stephanie Vie and Jennifer Roth Miller

> *"Let's catch that Dugtrio over there."*
> *"I can't believe you have a Tyranitar! I don't have enough candies to evolve. But I got a dragon scale so I have a Kingdra."*

Those unfamiliar with the augmented reality (AR) game *Pokémon Go* may not understand the above statements, but to game players, they are immediately recognizable. Dugtrio, Tyranitar, and Kingdra are characters in this popular game in which players capture and evolve Pokémon and battle in gyms. Meanwhile, players spin PokéStops, located near real-world points of interest, and receive Poké Balls (used to capture Pokémon), eggs that hatch new Pokémon, health potions, and other items.

Despite its dismissal by some as a simple casual game, *Pokémon Go* and similar AR games that rely on real-world location-based data remain intriguing case studies for scholars interested in the convergence of gameplay, privacy, and big data. Its gameplay depends on user-generated information about landmarks, local monuments' descriptions, and street-level navigation. As Barry Joseph states, "When you play *Pokémon Go*, you are playing Google Maps. And, the augmented reality that makes the gameplay so compelling, the tool behind the experience of co-presence, is big data" (2016). Such games also depend on socially networked environments for the fullest game experience—users must pick a team, battle others, and

DOI: 10.7330/9781646420315.c006

take over gyms to advance. These social elements combine with user-generated data for a game that depends on networks of people and their data.

Their reliance on AR and social networks means games like *Pokémon Go* present compelling quandaries for scholars interested in surveillance, social media, and game play. First, the privacy policies and terms of service for socially networked games are frequently problematic, and *Pokémon Go* is yet another example (see Beck et al. 2016; Vie 2014, 2016). A second compelling quandary is potential threats to personal safety; users have been harmed (e.g., muggings near PokéStops) and caught engaging in illegal activities like trespassing. Finally, many users may be unaware of terms-of-service clauses that waive important legal rights given that many fail to read these documents (see McDonald and Cranor 2008; Obar and Oeldorf-Hirsch 2018; Vie 2014, 2016). Yet despite potential issues, *Pokémon Go* has encouraged players to enjoy nature and engage in physical fitness and has brought users together in virtual communities supporting the game. Thus, a tension exists between the risks (privacy violations, surveillance, physical harm) and the benefits (increased physical fitness, social networking, and engagement with nature) the game provides.

This chapter assesses privacy and digital writing in social gaming spaces by examining *Pokémon Go* as a case study of AR games that bring together big data, privacy issues, and social networks. When considering privacy matters, this case study offers opportunities to question how written textual information is used in the game as a means to constrain individuals' privacy (e.g., written privacy policies and terms of service, textual descriptions of virtual-game landmarks that butt up against offline landmarks like churches or schools) and outside the game's socially networked space to critique gameplay elements (e.g., security experts' warnings about privacy issues in the game). These examples illustrate how writing educators can examine current examples of the ways textual composing circulates around privacy issues in augmented, networked games.

POKÉMON GO AND AUGMENTED REALITY

Released July 6, 2016, in thirty countries, *Pokémon Go* was down-loaded an estimated 7.5 million times in the United States in the first week. In 2018, more than 147 million monthly active global users were still readily capturing Pokémon (Phillips 2018). *Pokémon Go* is one of the first widely successful AR games, combining elements of the virtual-game world and the non-digital world and its geography. AR integrates the virtual and the physical for an enhanced, information-rich, contextual experience. When players catch Pokémon, they can turn on AR mode in-game, allowing them to see Pokémon in the real world—perhaps standing on a printer or hiding in backyard grasses. AR can be traced back as far as World War II and the British military's development of the Mark VIII Airborne Interception Radar Gunsighting project (Berryman 2012, 213). Corporate attention has been directed at AR since (see Berryman 2012; Roesner, Kohno, and Molnar 2014)—from Sutherland's head-mounted 3D display to Disney's Haunted Mansion ride to current AR games such as geocaching and *Ingress* to wearable AR like Google Glass. In particular, AR experiences exhibit six main characteristics: they sense properties about the real world, process in real time, overlay information to the user, provide contextual information, recognize and track real-world objects, and are mobile or wearable (University of Washington 2016).

AR offers many benefits and has been taken up in a variety of fields such as public health and exercise (see Althoff, White, and Horvitz 2016; Baranowski 2016; LeBlanc and Chaput 2017), medicine and surgery (see Mitrasinovic et al. 2015), libraries and museums (see Berryman 2012; Cyrus and Baggett 2012), recreation and parks (see Oakleaf 2015), and education (see Little 2016). AR offers users access to libraries of information overlaid upon the physical world, and indeed, AR may be the future of libraries (Berryman 2012). Additionally, gaming aspects such as sociality, fun factor, and purpose, such as exercise, often contribute to users' motivation to participate (see Kari 2016; Reinhardt and Heinig 2016).

However, the promise of technology and progress ideology have fostered an overwhelmingly uncritical acceptance of AR technology: Many users appear to have given up on privacy concerns that emerge as technology increasingly becomes central to daily life (Pedersen 2014, 16–18). Kenneth Eng describes the current tech economy as a freemium business model in which users receive complimentary app use in exchange for ads and advertising data (2016, 249–79). Users can pay to skip ads but nevertheless still provide data.[1] Nathan Hulsey and Joshua Reeves further describe the gift of play in exchange for surveillance and data, which becomes the only way to "access goods, build and maintain social relationships, and participate in politics" (2014, 389–400). Furthermore, AR has presented additional concerns such as intellectual property (copyright and logo infringement), free speech, physical safety, discrimination, and the environmental impact of data-storage issues (see Fink and Zagoria 2016; Klaus 2016; Tech Policy Lab 2016).

However, these concerns are not new but rather are an extension of the developing freemium model (see Brown 2016; Fink and Zagoria 2016; Hyman 2013; "*Pokémon Go* Caught Millions of Players and Their Data" 2016;). Photography, video recording, geolocation, and even emerging facial-recognition technology allow both users and developers (Neustaedter, Tang, and Judge 2013) to monitor participants. However, despite the fact that AR technology requires long-term access to personal data, AR may actually increase privacy and control with better detection of user authenticity and increased control settings. Ironically, facial-recognition technology may also prove to be the ultimate solution because faces of unwilling participants can be recognized and cross-referenced with their social networking privacy settings (Kotsios 2015).

Delphine Reinhardt and Christian Heinig surveyed participants of AR/geolocation-based crowdsourcing efforts and games and found they engaged freely regardless of concerns and that competition, status, fun, and goodwill motivated them most (2016, 27–36). Data collection via smartphone apps is sometimes perceived by participants to benefit the game, the community, cultural heritage (DeVan, *Penn State News*, January 1, 2017), and social good, showing that users frequently see data collection as beneficial until proven otherwise.

Alexander Clark and Matthew Clark argue that *Pokémon Go* is "the first mass market app that fully transcends the virtual, the spatial, the social, and the physical" (2016, 1–3). In the next section, we consider case studies from *Pokémon Go* focusing on privacy policies and terms of service, as well as written responses critiquing the game's privacy issues. These case studies illustrate how digital writing provides a means for surveillance to prosper and also gives individuals a means of resistance to fight back against privacy violations or inappropriate surveillance. Thus, readers may see how privacy matters that when AR and socially networked games have a powerful means to both exploit users' individual private data and offer resistance to said privacy exploitation.

CASE STUDY 1: *POKÉMON GO'S* TERMS-OF-SERVICE AND PRIVACY POLICIES

Most digital games require users to agree to terms of service (ToS), privacy policies (PP), and/or end-user licensing agreements (EULAs). ToS generally accompany apps installed on mobile devices, while EULAs accompany downloaded computer software. PP, often separate but sometimes embedded within ToS, address users' private data—its capture, storage, and circulation, and whether the user can petition to have the data deleted or released.

ToS and PP are often complex, lengthy, and highly specific, requiring much text to cover all required aspects related to the product; additionally, the authors must ensure their legality. Yet for all the time put into crafting ToS or PP documents, few end users read them.[2] Multiple studies have inserted ridiculous clauses into ToS and PP documents purposefully to test whether users read them. Inevitably, few do, leading to end users who agree to give up their souls or first-born children (see Feltman, *Washington Post*, September 29, 2014; Obar and Oeldorf-Hirsch 2018).

However, other ToS are far less overt and perhaps more insidious; they ask users to give up their rights to content such as text, photographs or likenesses, music, and other elements many might push against if they were more fully aware of the clauses' existence. Natasha Singer considers several of these cases, such as Craigslist, for which users give the site the right to "copy, perform, display, distribute, prepare derivative works from (including, without limitation, incorporating into other works) and otherwise use any content that [they] post" (2014). At the height of the MySpace craze, when many musicians placed their catalogues on MySpace to gain wider audiences, musician Billy Bragg realized he signed away his music rights once he accepted the site's ToS; realizing this, he protested and successfully fought for MySpace to change its ToS (Vie 2008). As Casey Feisler, Cliff Lampe, and Amy Bruckman have noted, "Policy can be as powerful a design agent as technology, so understanding user impressions of policy is essential to the growth of these environments. However, its role is often considered only as an afterthought or when it becomes a problem" (2016, 1–12). That is, users exhibit concern and outrage after the fact; they frequently don't read ToS and PP to preemptively address concerns about privacy, data collection and use, or surveillance.

In the case of *Pokémon Go*, this same phenomenon occurs. Two aspects of *Pokémon Go* are discussed in this case-study section: the ToS, as well as application permissions and the attendant PP. This game's ToS were last updated May 15, 2019 (at the time of this writing); the initial game rollout date was July 6, 2016. Thus, the ToS were not updated for the three years following the game's rollout. The PP, however, was updated multiple times (at the time of this writing) in response to ongoing critiques surrounding users' personal-data privacy. Amid the initial flurry of interest in *Pokémon Go*, several prominent websites published critiques of the PP once it was noticed that the app requested access to a player's Google calendar, photos, and other elements when using Apple's iOS. Adam Reeve (a security analytics employee) posted on Tumblr that "to play the game you need an account. Weirdly, Niantic won't let you just create one—you need to sign in with an existing account from one of two services—the Pokémon.com website or Google. Now the Pokémon site is for some reason not accepting new signups right now so if you're not already registered there you'll need to use a Google account—and that's where the fun begins" (2016).

Reeve continues by noting that the requirement to sign in using Google, forcing users to connect through a particular provider, exposed them to a far broader permissions request than anticipated. That is, after a player logged in, the app said, "*Pokémon Go* has full access to your Google account"—meaning *Pokémon Go* and Niantic could read the user's emails, send email as the user, access and delete all Google Drive documents, look at a user's search history and Maps navigation history, access all photos (including private photos) in Google Photos, and potentially access other sites and services requiring Gmail to authenticate (2016). Importantly, the app did not provide a pop-up notification identifying these access levels; instead, a user had to log in to Google itself and look at the permissions granted to each app (Frank 2016). Reeve notes that he deleted the app immediately, stating "I wish I could play, it looks like great fun, but there's no way it's worth the risk."

For what it's worth, Niantic—developers of *Pokémon Go*— quickly responded once these concerns were raised. Reaching out directly via social media, Niantic stated:

> We recently discovered that the *Pokémon GO* account creation process on iOS erroneously requests full access permission for the user's Google account. . . . Once we became aware of this error, we began working on a client-side fix to request permission for only basic Google profile information, in line with the data that we actually access. Google has verified that no other information has been received or accessed by *Pokémon GO* or Niantic. Google will soon reduce *Pokémon GO*'s permission to only the basic profile data that *Pokémon GO* needs, and users do not need to take any actions themselves. (Frank 2016)[3]

However, this case study raises important questions: What if users had not realized quickly that Niantic and *Pokémon Go* had these levels of access? What if instead *Pokémon Go* users—as is typical—had not read the ToS or PP and not logged in to Google to check the app's permissions? In other words, it is laudable that a security analytics worker noticed within two days of the app's launch that the permissions were of concern and then posted via social media rapidly to circulate this information, but given how infrequently users preemptively read ToS and PP or examine app permissions, this case study could have gone differently. Similarly, Niantic explained this overreach as a coding mistake, and others examining the code agreed it appeared Niantic was not maliciously requesting such permissions (Rubenstein 2016). Once again, though, the outcome could have been different if an app developer had devious inclinations and wanted to use code (a language not all of us understand deeply) to gather information for malicious intent. For example, cybercriminals often use software bundled with keyloggers to record a user's keystrokes, thereby capturing emails, passwords, credit-card numbers, and other data that can be used with criminal intent (Grebennikov 2007). As Marissa Lang states in a July 12, 2016, article in the *San Francisco Chronicle*, "Developers routinely ask for access to more than what they need, and users rarely refuse them when scrambling to access a hot new app or game."

While *Pokémon Go* responded rapidly to permissions issues, the ToS remain another lingering concern. Its ToS, like many others, include language about binding legal arbitration. In this case, unless players opt out within the first thirty days of using the app, they concede to Niantic's statement about arbitration:

ARBITRATION NOTICE: EXCEPT IF YOU OPT OUT AND EXCEPT FOR CERTAIN TYPES OF DISPUTES DESCRIBED IN THE "AGREEMENT TO ARBITRATE" SECTION BELOW, YOU AGREE THAT DISPUTES BETWEEN YOU AND NIANTIC WILL BE RESOLVED BY BINDING, INDIVIDUAL ARBITRATION, AND YOU ARE WAIVING YOUR RIGHT TO A TRIAL BY JURY OR TO PARTICIPATE AS A PLAINTIFF OR CLASS MEMBER IN ANY PURPORTED CLASS ACTION OR REPRESENTATIVE PROCEEDING. (Lomas 2016; emphasis and capitalization in the original)

Thus Niantic has effectively coerced many players, by virtue of their unlikeliness to read the ToS and/or understand what it means to waive one's right to trial by jury, into binding arbitration. Rob Price illustrates one potential problematic scenario: "If the company was hacked, say, and all of its users' data got stolen, then these users wouldn't be able to collectively bring a case against the company" (2016). In a July 14, 2016, post to the *Consumerist* blog, Chris Morran expanded: "Rather than have to answer for the totality of the error, the company would only have to face those few users who take the time—and have the resources—to bring a case before an arbitrator" (2016). This is not unique to *Pokémon Go*; many ToS include language about binding arbitration, and many users opt in unknowingly because they fail to read the ToS. And this issue is one that should be of concern for many of us as we navigate a world increasingly mediated by socially networked technologies, including games, applications, and social media platforms.

Michael Rustad et al. argue that such arbitration clauses "contravene many of the basic principles deemed indispensable for a fundamentally fair process for consumers to obtain civil recourse for recognized torts and remedies for contract disputes. Congress needs to prohibit predispute mandatory arbitration clauses in terms of service agreements and privacy policies" (2012, 644). In a 2011 Senate hearing, Lori Swanson, attorney general in St. Paul, Minnesota, described how her office filed a lawsuit against the National Arbitration Forum in 2009 after finding this forum was deceptive in its representations to clients. Specifically, it went to lengths to appear independent, neutral, and impartial, but in fact it

> had extensive ties to the collection industry and was, in essence, an arm of the collection industry . . . work[ing] behind the scenes . . . against the interests of ordinary consumers to convince credit card companies and other debt buyers and other corporations to insert mandatory pre-dispute arbitration clauses into . . . contracts and then to appoint the forum to decide the disputes, essentially putting itself as part of the collection process (*Arbitration* 2011).

Swanson's comments illustrate that—far from neutral entities—many arbitration forums serve the interests of corporations, not individuals.

Much like *Pokémon Go*—a socially networked app—other social media platforms rely on similar embedded arbitration clauses or include a thirty-day opt-out window. For instance, Instagram revised its terms of use in 2013, requiring users to enter arbitration and prohibiting them from challenging the ToU by initiating or joining class-action lawsuits or class-wide arbitration (Rustad and Koenig 2014). Unlike *Pokémon Go* users, however, Instagram users could not simply write to the company and opt out; instead, they had to delete the app and quit using it within one month of beginning use (Rustad and Koenig 2014).

Echoing earlier discussions of the difficulty of reading and accessing ToS in this chapter, Rustad and Thomas Koenig observe that Instagram's opt-out clause "is labeled inconspicuously and is entombed 3689 words (sixty-one paragraphs) into a TOU that lacks an index or any other navigational guide," and further, "the TOU's truncated discussion makes no mention that the pre-dispute mandatory arbitration clause extinguishes the user's Seventh Amendment right to a civil jury trial and the user's right to liberal discovery" (2014, 1431–517). Increasingly, companies create ways to coerce individuals to accept binding arbitration not through clicking on "I agree" for a ToS or ToU but instead by doing something as ubiquitous as clicking Like on a company's Facebook page or downloading a coupon. Emily Canis compares the cases of General Mills and AOL, who incorporated ToS language allowing consumers to be bound by mandatory arbitration simply by interacting with the companies online (2015, 135–36). Canis also notes that recent Supreme Court decisions regarding consumer challenges to such ToS have generally been settled in favor of the company, not the consumer, highlighting users' vulnerability. In this collection, Christina Cedillo (chapter 7) remarks that "surveillance encourages people to regulate themselves and others to maintain the status quo."

We are not making any argument for or against arbitration itself; that is beyond the scope of our analysis. Instead, our concern is that *Pokémon Go,* like many other socially mediated apps, relies on ToS and PP that are lengthy, are not typically read by consumers, are not frequently fully understood, and include mandatory arbitration requirements that have, as illustrated here, been critiqued by multiple law and ethics scholars, as well as senators and representatives. These case studies of *Pokémon Go*'s ToS and PP are intended to showcase how writing in a digital age is often used by corporations to obfuscate individuals' rights, pointing to the continued necessity for digital rhetoric scholars to attend to the implications of such documents for personal legal rights, as well as rights to collectively resist surveillance or breaches of personal data.

DIGITAL WRITING AS RESISTANCE: OPTING OUT AND FIGHTING BACK

The examples of overstepping consumers' privacy boundaries and coercion into mandatory arbitration agreements are not unique to this game. Instead, we present them as case studies because of two important elements. One is that *Pokémon Go* is, quite simply, quotidian. It's a relatively inoffensive game most would view as a casual game, easy to pick up and put down, not particularly difficult to play. Because it is commonplace, *Pokémon Go* is not a technology most would assume is connected to significant questions around privacy, surveillance, or consumer data. And yet it, like so many other seemingly insignificant technologies (such as Facebook Likes, mobile games, and digital coupons), indeed has import when we consider how valuable most of us consider our personal privacy, our digital data, and our legal rights.

Second, *Pokémon Go* illustrates something of particular interest to digital rhetoricians and writing scholars, and that is its connection to digital writing as resistance. The circulation of writing in digital spaces (the game app itself, the ToS and PP hosted online, written posts online about the ToS and PP, legal cases such as *Beckman v. Niantic Inc.,* etc.) that connects to privacy, user-generated data, surveillance, and the law showcases the power of such composing to both constrain individuals' rights and create spaces for individuals to resist abuses of power. While it is beyond the scope of this chapter to delve deeply into other associated ways digital writing has been used to either establish Niantic's abilities to surveil players or harvest their data, we mention a few moments in passing to more broadly showcase how digital writing is a major player in considerations of privacy, surveillance, and individual agency.

For example, in his analysis of the game's code on both Android and iOS devices, Vincent Lawson determined that forensic analysis of said code could be used by law enforcement "to create a timeline for user activity, coordinates for encounters to create a travel route, and various user and application metrics like account user name, date the app was last opened, and date the app was last closed" (2016, 57), all data that could be subpoenaed and used in court to make claims about an individual's whereabouts or behaviors at a particular time. Also, to return to the discussion of AR and *Pokémon Go* addressed earlier, AR—which is literally written into the game's code—has led to multiple written explorations of the relationship among AR, the offline world, and trespassing. The 2016 case *Marder v. Niantic Inc.* centered around a California homeowner who sued Niantic because of its "flagrant disregard for the foreseeable consequences of populating the real world with virtual Pokémon without seeking the permission of property owners" (*Marder v. Niantic* 2016). Other written documents have addressed the ramifications of AR games that entice players to move physically into offline spaces that may be contested, like cemeteries, public schools, and homeowners' yards (see Kochan 2017). As Donald Kochan argues, "Augmented reality not only tests the law but also helps us recognize the limitations of the law" (2017).

More broadly, we maintain that *Pokémon Go*, a socially networked AR game, pushes against the boundaries of written digital discourse; through its constraints of, and straining against, such boundaries, it asks us to consider the convergence of augmented and virtual reality, corporations' and individuals' rights, and the implications of privacy, surveillance, and digital data that circulate through the game and the paratextual writing surrounding it. As such games are only poised to become more popular in coming years, scholars must continue considering the powerful role digital and networked writing plays in determining legal, moral, and ethical boundaries to our movement in said games.

NOTES

1. See Timothy Amidon and Jessica Reyman (2014) for a rich discussion of user contributions and ownership of data in the social web. Also consult Colleen Reilly's chapter in this volume for her discussion of the exchanges that occur behind the scenes of online advertising and several assignments that can be adapted for the college writing classroom that encourage students to grapple with the implications of their online activities and their connections to tracking and surveillance.

2. See, for example, Dustin Edwards's chapter in this volume, which analyzes the Mywellness Cloud platform vis-à-vis both the company's terms-of-service document and its privacy policy, as well as the circulation of user data through various channels (e.g., fiber-optic cables) and the ways such personal data thus literally flows through different third parties and across varied geographical locations (77).

3. Interestingly, this statement is no longer accessible at all through Niantic's own website; only copies referenced on various blogs and social media remain as a record.

REFERENCES

Althoff, Tim, Ryen W. White, and Eric Horvitz. 2016. "Influence of *Pokémon Go* on Physical Activity: Study and Implications." *Journal of Medical Internet Research* 18 (12), e315: 1–14.

Amidon, Timothy R., and Jessica Reyman. 2014. "Authorship and Ownership of User Contributions on the Social Web." In *Cultures of Copyright*, edited by Dànielle Nicole DeVoss and Martine Courant Rife, 108–24. New York: Peter Lang.

Arbitration: Is It Fair When Forced?: Hearing on S. 987 and S. 1652 Before the Senate Committee on the Judiciary. 2011. *112th Congress.* October 13. https://www .govinfo.gov/content/pkg/CHRG-112shrg71582/pdf/CHRG-112shrg71582 .pdf.

"Augmented Reality: A Technology and Policy Primer." 2016. *University of Washington.* Accessed May 15, 2016.

Baranowski, Tom. 2016. "*Pokémon Go,* Go, Go, Gone?" *Games for Health Journal: Research, Development, and Clinical Applications* 5 (5): 293–94.

Beck, Estee N., Angela Crow, Heidi A. McKee, Colleen A. Reilly, Jennifer deWinter, Stephanie Vie, Laura Gonzales, and Dànielle Nicole DeVoss. 2016. "Writing in an Age of Surveillance, Privacy, and Net Neutrality." *Kairos: A Journal of Rhetoric, Technology, and Pedagogy* 20 (2). http://kairos.technorhetoric.net/20.2/topoi/beck-et-al/beck.html.

Beckman v. Niantic Inc. 2016. Circuit Court of the Fifteenth Judicial Circuit in and for Palm Beach County, Florida. http://digitalcommons.law.scu.edu/cgi/viewcontent.cgi?article=2468&context=historical.

Berryman, Donna. 2012. "Augmented Reality: A Review." *Medical Reference Services Quarterly* 31 (2): 212–18. doi:10.1080/02763869.2012.670604.

Brown, Bob. 2016. "*Pokémon Go* Maker Addresses Google Account Access Scare." *Network World*, July 12. http://www.networkworld.com/article/3094416/mobile-wireless/pokemon-go-maker-addresses-google-account-access-scare.html.

Canis, Emily. 2015. "One 'Like' Away: Mandatory Arbitration for Consumers." *George Mason University Civil Rights Law Journal* 26 (1): 127–55.

Clark, Alexander M., and Matthew T. G. Clark. 2016. "*Pokémon Go* and Research: Qualitative, Mixed Methods Research, and the Supercomplexity of Interventions." *International Journal of Qualitative Methods* 15 (1): 1–3.

Cyrus, John W., and Mark P. Baggett. 2012. "Mobile Technology: Implications for Privacy and Librarianship." *Reference Librarian* 53 (3): 284–96. doi:10.1080/02763877.2012.678765.

Eng, Kenneth W. 2016. "Content Creators, Virtual Goods: Who Owns Virtual Property?" *Cardozo Arts & Entertainment Law Journal* 34 (1): 249–79.

Feisler, Casey, Cliff Lampe, and Amy S. Bruckman. 2016. "Reality and Perception of Copyright Terms of Service for Online Content Creation." In *Proceedings of the 16th Conference on Computer-Supported Cooperative Work and Social Computing*, 1–12. New York: Association for Computing Machinery.

Fink, David E., and Jamie N. Zagoria. 2016. "VR and AR in a Real World." *Entertainment & Sports Lawyer* 33 (1): 1–79.

Frank, Allegra. 2016. "*Pokémon Go* Raises Security Concerns among Google Users (Update)." *Polygon*, July 11. http://www.polygon.com/2016/7/11/12151442/Pokémon-go-security-risk-data-information-ios-android.

Grebennikov, Nikolas. 2007. "Keyloggers: How They Work and How to Detect Them (Part 1)." *SecureList*, March 29. https://securelist.com/analysis/publications/36138/keyloggers-how-they-work-and-how-to-detect-them-part-1/.

Hulsey, Nathan, and Joshua Reeves. 2014. "The Gift That Keeps on Giving: Google, *Ingress*, and the Gift of Surveillance." *Surveillance & Society* 12 (3): 389–400.

Hyman, Paul. 2013. "Augmented-Reality Glasses Bring Cloud Security into Sharp Focus." *Communications of the ACM* 56 (6): 18–20. doi:10.1145/2461256.2461264.

Joseph, Barry. 2016. "The Secret Sauce in *Pokémon Go*: Big Data." DML Central. https://dmlcentral.net/secret-sauce-Pokémon-go/.

Kari, Tuomas. 2016. "*Pokémon Go* 2016: Exploring Situational Contexts of Critical Incidents in Augmented Reality." *Journal of Virtual Worlds Research* 9 (3): 1–12.

Klaus, Jeff. 2016. "The Bandwidth Paradox: How *Pokémon Go* Pushes Connectivity Boundaries and Data Center Demands." *Database Trends & Applications* 30 (5): 11–12.

Kochan, Donald J. 2017. "Playing with Real Property Inside Augmented Reality: *Pokémon Go*, Trespass, and Law's Limitations." *Whittier Law Review* 38 (2): 70–94.

Kotsios, Andreas. 2015. "Privacy in an Augmented Reality." *International Journal of Law & Information Technology* 23 (2): 157–85. doi:10.1093/ijlit/eav003.

Lawson, Vincent. 2016. "A Forensic Examination of *Pokémon Go*." Master's thesis, Utica College.

LeBlanc, Allana G., and Jean-Philippe Chaput. 2017. "Commentary: *Pokémon Go*: A Game Changer for the Physical Inactivity Crisis?" *Preventive Medicine* 101: 1–2. doi:10.1016/j.ypmed.2016.11.012.

Little, Catherine. 2016. "Gotta Catch 'Em All: Teaching with *Pokémon Go*." *Teach* (September/October): 25–27.

Lomas, Natasha. 2016. "*Pokemon Go* T&Cs Strip Users of Legal Rights." TechCrunch, July 17. https://techcrunch.com/2016/07/17/pokemon-go-tcs-strip-users-of-legal-rights/.

Marder v. Niantic. 2016. "Class Action Complaint: Marder v. Niantic, Inc." United States District Court Northern District of California. http://online.wsj.com/public/resources/documents/2016_0802_pokemon_lawsuit.pdf.

McDonald, Aleecia M., and Lorrie Faith Cranor. 2008. "The Cost of Reading Privacy Policies." *I/S: A Journal of Law and Policy for the Information Society* 4 (3): 543–68.

Mitrasinovic, Stefan, Elvis Camacho, Nirali Trivedi, Julia Logan, Colson Campbell, Robert Zilinyi, Bryan Lieber, Eliza Bruce, Blake Taylor, David Martineau, Emmanuel L. P. Dumont, Geoff Appelboom, and E. Sander Connolly Jr. 2015. "Clinical and Surgical Applications of Smart Glasses." *Technology & Health Care* 23 (4): 381–401. doi:10.3233/THC-150910.

Neustaedter, Carman, Anthony Tang, and Tejinder K. Judge. 2013. "Creating Scalable Location-Based Games: Lessons from Geocaching." *Personal & Ubiquitous Computing* 17 (2): 335–49.

Oakleaf, Linda. 2015. "A Virtual War: Augmented Reality Comes to Our Parks with *Ingress*." *Parks & Recreation* 50 (4): 16.

Obar, Jonathan A., and Anne Oeldorf-Hirsch. 2018. "The Biggest Lie on the Internet: Ignoring the Privacy Policies and Terms of Service Policies of Social Networking Services." *Information, Communication, and Society* 23 (1): 128–47. https://doi.org/10.1080/1369118X.2018.1486870.

Pedersen, Isabel. 2014. "Are Wearables Really Ready to Wear?" *IEEE Technology & Society Magazine* 33 (2): 16–18.

Phillips, Tom. 2018. "*Pokemon Go* Active Player Count Highest since 2016 Summer Launch." Eurogamer. Accessed June 27, 2018. https://www.eurogamer.net/articles/2018-06-27-pokemon-go-player-count-at-highest-since-2016-summer-launch.

"*Pokémon Go* Caught Millions of Players and Their Data." 2016. *Information Management Journal* 50 (5): 12.

"Pokémon GO Terms of Service." 2016. Niantic Labs, July 1. https://www.nianticlabs.com/terms/Pokémongo/en.

Price, Rob. 2016. "An Obscure Clause in *Pokémon Go*'s Terms-and-Conditions Signs Away Your Right to a Jury Trial." Business Insider, July 18. http://www .businessinsider.com/pokmon-go-terms-of-service-signs-away-users-right-to -trial-class-action-lawsuit-forced-arbitration-2016-7.

Reeve, Adam. 2016. Tumblr, "*Pokémon Go* Is a Huge Security Risk." http:// adamreeve.tumblr.com/post/147120922009/Pokémon-go-is-a-huge-security -risk.

Reinhardt, Delphine, and Christian Heinig. 2016. "Survey-Based Exploration of Attitudes to Participatory Sensing Tasks in Location-Based Gaming Communities." *Pervasive and Mobile Computing* 27 (April): 27–36.

Roesner, Franziska, Tadayoshi Kohno, and David Molnar. 2014. "Security and Privacy for Augmented Reality Systems." *Communications of the ACM* 57 (4): 88–96.

Rubenstein, Ari. 2016. "Pokémon Tokens." GitHub Gist. https://gist.github .com/arirubinstein/fd5453537436a8757266f908c3e41538.

Rustad, Michael L., Richard Buckingham, Diane D'Angelo, and Katherine Durlacher. 2012. "An Empirical Study of Predispute Mandatory Arbitration Clauses in Social Media Terms of Service Agreements." *University of Arkansas Little Rock Law Review* 34 (4): 643–88.

Rustad, Michael L., and Thomas H. Koenig. 2014. "Wolves of the World Wide Web: Reforming Social Networks' Contracting Practices." *Wake Forest Law Review* 49: 1431–1517.

Singer, Natasha. 2014. "Didn't Read Those Terms of Service? Here's What You Agreed to Give Up." *Bits (blog), New York Times*. April 28. https://bits.blogs .nytimes.com/2014/04/28/didnt-read-those-terms-of-service-heres-what -you-agreed-to-give-up/?_r=0.

University of Washington Tech Policy Lab. 2016. *Augmented Reality: A Technology and Policy Primer*. http://techpolicylab.org/wp-content/uploads/2016/02/ Augmented_Reality_Primer-TechPolicyLab.pdf.

Vie, Stephanie. 2008. "'I Gave My Rights Away for a Song': How Billy Bragg Persuaded MySpace to Change Its Tune on Ownership." In *The Business of Entertainment: Popular Music*, edited by Robert Praeger, 107–19. Santa Barbara: ABC-Clio.

Vie, Stephanie. 2014. "'You Are How You Play': Privacy Policies and Data Mining in Social Networking Games." In *Computer Games and Technical Communication*, edited by Jennifer deWinter and Ryan Moeller, 171–87. New York: Ashgate.

Vie, Stephanie. 2016. "Policies, Terms of Service, and Social Networking Games." In *Video Game Policy: Production, Distribution, and Consumption*, edited by Steven Conway and Jennifer deWinter, 54–67. New York: Routledge.

PART III

Surveillance and Culture

7

THE PERILS OF THE PUBLIC PROFESSORIATE
On Surveillance, Social Media, and Identity-Avoidant Frameworks

Christina V. Cedillo

Our lives are constantly segmented, analyzed, and transmuted into usable bits of data. As people participate in even the most pedestrian activities, they divulge information about themselves and allow institutional entities to authenticate their identities. These seemingly innocuous activities sustain surveillance, a "political technology of population management" that relies on bodily regulation (Ceyhan 2012, 40) and manifests as "an ambivalent mix of freedom and control, security and uncertainty" (Friesen, Feenberg and Smith 2009, 84). Surveillance encourages people to regulate themselves and others to maintain the status quo. Surveillance technologies greatly sway scholarly activity: online programs monitor academic integrity[1] while social media transform how academics share information, at times in adverse ways.

Here, I examine three cases of Twitter use that reveal how surveillance fosters the online vulnerability of academics from minoritized communities. I argue that surveillance's reliance on datafication and dataveillance bolsters social regulation targeting members of vulnerable populations through identity avoidance, the deliberate erasure of identity in social interactions. Identity-avoidant frameworks function to shift blame onto the targets of bigotry. These frameworks connect to ingrained optic technologies habituated by historical surveillance practices[2] that have their origins in colonial classification, highlighting their

DOI: 10.7330/9781646420315.c007

ideological aim—the preservation of social hierarchies. The representation and regulation enabled by these processes bolster identity-avoidant frameworks online that affect individuals marked by marginalized identities. In examining Twitter harassment cases involving academics Steven Salaita, Saida Grundy, and Daniel Brewster, I aim to show how modes of knowing associated with surveillance bolster identity-avoidant frameworks, allowing individuals to be harassed due to their identities even as their harassers claim such attacks are not based in prejudice.

The cases of Salaita, Grundy, and Brewster illustrate how surveillance and identity avoidance permit detractors to censure individuals using the very bigotries their targets seek to contest. Twitter proves an ideal platform for examining how online identity segmentation bolsters already-present prejudices. Tweets function through rhetorical reduction: a person becomes a monodimensional persona on a profile, read vis-à-vis taxonomic identity markers interpreted as the individual's entire person and perspective. Social media do not reinvent but reinscribe these surveillance paradigms. Social media ethos construction coincides with the selective representation identity-avoidant frameworks and dataveillance demand.[3] Thus, popular reliance on datafication and dataveillance as habituated ways of knowing presents liabilities for members of marginalized groups.

"UN/SEEING": SURVEILLANCE AND IDENTITY-AVOIDANT FRAMEWORKS

Surveillance is theorized as an "impersonal . . . generic watching of the population-at-large" or targeted monitoring for particular aims (Jenkins 2012, 162–63; van Dijck 2014, 205). In either case, surveillance proves powerful and useful to social control. The data surveillance makes available become meaningful through *dataveillance*, which determines what information proves useful and relevant in a given context, what interpretational frameworks are to be used and to what end. Dataveillance is a powerful, habituated optic technology with roots in colonialism that uses representation as regulation of a large population (van Dijck 2014, 197–208); it creates social categories and provides epistemic apparatus for engaging with the world (Levi and Wall 2004 quoted in Amoore and Goede 2005, 151; Lupton and Williamson 2017, 3).

The driving force behind dataveillance is data segmentation, which establishes what elements of identity can be controlled, monitored, analyzed, and substituted for the whole person (Lyon 2001; Plummer 1974, 33–37). In the digital world, segmentation relies on taxonomies maintained by architects and designers, who determine how categories are delineated and how social regulation takes place through the preservation of identity categories by individual, communal, or corporate users. For example, a recent *ProPublica* review of Facebook's policy on hate speech notes that the platform's demarcation of population subsets protects racist speech while flagging antiracist posts (Angwin and Grassegger 2017; Develin, *Guardian*, April 13, 2017). Surveillance influences media design, which, in turn, influences how surveillance is enacted via the platform.

Surveillance, dataveillance, and data segmentation are deployed by dominant groups to regulate subjugated populations and establish the dominant groups' power vis-à-vis epistemic authority. On social media, these technologies expedite such regulation and authorization through their substantiation of *identity-avoidant frameworks*, paradigms that paradoxically rely on constructs of identity to deny the salience and material effects of these constructs. *Colorblindness*, defined as the supposed inability to "see" race, allows privileged individuals to claim they do not perceive racial difference, reinforcing myths of meritocracy and progress. Moreover, the term's central analogy signals the privilege behind a direct refusal to contend with race while depending on deficit views of disabled people (Annamma, Jackson, and Morrison 2017, 153).[4] Other identity-avoidant arguments suggest that not wanting members of the queer community to be too visible or have equal marriage rights is not homophobia but a protection of traditional values. Another kind claims women have a right to work but not to earn as much as men because a man tends to be a family's primary breadwinner.

Identity-avoidance frameworks merged with surveillance technologies affect how individuals are perceived on social media, easily rendering a marginalized person's identity as a priori proof of fallibility. Identity avoidance relies on "un/seeing" difference, meaning those details that dataveillance uses to categorize people—and the perspectives that authorize their use—are implicitly accepted as valid and bias free. When targets of systemic violence cite difference as grounds for discrimination, dominant-culture perspectives can frame them as intolerant aggressors who invoke bigotry where there is none to be found, marking them as the "real" bigots. Paradoxically, members of marginalized communities are assumed only too willing to claim discrimination due to their identities (for instance, by "playing the race card") even as forms of discrimination associated with said identities are denied. A supposed tendency to claim victimization becomes yet another means for surveilling and circumscribing already-vulnerable populations. This powerful combination of identity avoidance and surveillance played a fundamental role in the online harassment of Salaita, Grundy, and Brewster.

SURVEILLANCE, SOCIAL MEDIA, AND SOCIAL CONTROL

Surveillance technologies are not recent inventions of the digital age. As decolonial critics like Walter Mignolo, Aníbal Quijano, and Linda Tuhiwai Smith explain, colonizers have long relied on models of power that reconfigure reality using geographic, biological, and academic sorting (Mignolo 2003; Quijano 2000, 533–80; Smith 2013). For centuries, colonial powers have used dataveillance to classify individuals into identifiable branded groups and encourage submission to organizational schemes that uphold such categorization. Histories of datafication and dataveillance reveal social control as the fundamental aim behind the development of these tools. For example, fingerprinting was first used in India (in 1858) to keep track of prisoners and colonial pensioners before being instituted in England as a means of largescale oversight, a transposing of technology from a colonized population to the general population of the colonial nation-state. Technicians effectively "summarized, represented in miniature, segmented and translated" individuals into representations accepted by most people as the norm (Sa'di 2012, 152).

In the online realm, these tools bolster the use of prejudicial lenses so ingrained in the popular episteme that their promoted biases go unnoticed and unquestioned. Social media encourage users to interpret the world through their design frameworks and influence how surveillance is enacted based on users' responses to and through the platform. While many users assume "social traffic flows through neutral technological channels" (van Dijck 2014, 199), an examination of Twitter use by harassed academics and their harassers discussed here demonstrates this neutrality is certainly not the case.

Twitter's dependence on data segmentation plays directly into the segmentation processes required by surveillance and dataveillance. Tweets are signifying units that do not contain all the meaning they convey: they link to other tweets, stories, users, and platforms. When users wish to articulate thoughts that require more space, they can publish a series of tweets using numbers to indicate the number of tweets in a thread, use plus signs, or respond directly to their previous posts. Hashtags allow users to search for select topics or their own archives. Because Twitter users often maintain public profiles, allowing them to gain thousands, even millions, of followers, every follower can reply and retweet their posts. In turn, so can their followers, with whom the original person posting may never even interact. This setup of "bleeding" units of meaning, easily lifted by strangers from the confines of their original contexts, creates the perfect storm for controversy.

Twitter also operates through synecdochal specularity, or a reliance on "a representation, a piece that represents a whole; or even a whole that contains its represented part" (Villanueva 2006, 15). This reduction serves a useful purpose in digital contexts by honing focus on select metrics (Gandy 2012, 140). This reduction demands "a new abstraction" that renders other information about users less conspicuous and therefore less important (Manovich 2008, 5). Furthermore, Twitter provides "a real-time collection of people's ideas and comments that is a gold mine for business and corporations" (Cross 2011, 57). This highly exploitable setup has important consequences for how people are read online.

Because many accounts are set to public, they are readily accessible for data mining, meaning the data tendered by tweets is used by corporate and political entities to influence the public's future choices regarding trends, topics, and interpretive lenses (Indiana University 2013). Through amusing features like quizzes and surveys, users become conditioned to provide information or access to their profiles for free. This "controllable information," the data profiles assembled through the tracking of virtual patterns of behavior (Beck 2015, 127–28), serves as the basis for further dataveillance and technological development. It also informs life beyond the digital realm, "extending" bodies to include trackable bits of data that "do not precisely belong to our body" but nevertheless are "indices of our bodily presence that track us, and for which we can be held responsible" (Friesen, Feenberg, and Smith 2009, 86–87). The profiling made possible by tracking sorts users into demographic groups with whom they themselves may or may not identify. This point matters because the categorization of human beings "necessarily contributes to how we treat them" and "put them in their place" in any society (Jenkins 2012, 160). In the case of Twitter, its organizational structure openly demands this special confluence of hypervisibility and erasure, uniquely positioning this platform as a space where forms of hostility aimed at Salaita, Grundy, and Brewster thrive, as I show below.

Steven Salaita

In August 2014, the University of Illinois Urbana–Champaign (UIUC) withdrew a job offer made to Steven Salaita, a scholar of Indigenous and Arab studies, after he published several tweets critical of Israel and its war with Hamas that sparked an uproar within the conservative blogosphere. Salaita, who identifies as Palestinian American and whose research interests include decoloniality and Palestine, had been offered a job in UIUC's American Indian studies program the previous October. In August, then-chancellor Phyllis Wise informed him his appointment would not go before the university's board of trustees, a decision that led to legal proceedings and provoked intense debate over the limits of academic freedom. Following a tweet in which he wished settlers of the West Bank "would go missing" that came soon after the kidnapping and subsequent killing of three Israeli teenagers, angry voices called for his deportation and even his execution for his perceived hatred of Jewish people. UIUC professor and former president of the American Association of University Professors Cary Nelson denounced Salaita's posts, stating that the tweets promoted "anti-Semitism" and were "almost a solicitation of violence" (Cohen, *Chicago Tribune*, August 14, 2014).

Datafication and dataveillance played a major role in how Salaita's online audiences interpreted his identity and his commentary. They enabled identity avoidance's paradoxical hypervisibility and erasure of specific identity markers to brand him a dangerous academic. Salaita's public tweets reached many different audiences. Those familiar with his research recognized how his identity informed his reaction to current events. Oftentimes, decolonial scholars focus on the political and ideological contexts affecting members of their own communities; not surprisingly, Salaita examines settler colonialism in Israel and the United States (Salaita 2006). In both these political settings, a disavowal of the settler colonialist character of the state has made it difficult to advocate for decolonial endeavors (Veracini 2010, 207). It is crucial to note this denial because it frames those who work toward decolonialization, or argue for its necessity as a critical lens for interpreting political situations, as nonconformists or troublemakers. While most of Salaita's supporters read his remarks through the lens of his decolonial scholarship and anger at the ongoing colonization of Palestine, users who denied or were uninformed about the settler-colonial situation focused on his "suspect" ethnic identity to typecast Salaita as an Islamophobic stereotype.

Because he is a Palestinian American, his identity was segmented and reduced so the one marker his detractors focused on was his affinity with a nation whose status is typically regarded by Western audiences as questionable or aggressive rather than resistant. Longstanding Orientalist tendencies cast Middle Eastern and Muslim identity as Other (see Said 1979). Furthermore, the significant place of 9/11 in the US imaginary has not only led to increased violence against Muslims and Middle Easterners but obfuscates the institutional structures of inequality that give rise to such violence in the first place (Naber 2008, 3). Salaita was framed as a foreign threat, a reduction that seemingly gave credence to his detractors' Islamophobic viewpoints. His tweets provided the necessary "proof" that Palestinians are cruel and anti-Semitic. Thus, demands that he be deported and accusations of malice could be framed as a defense of another vulnerable group, Jewish people, rather than an identity-based attack. Through the lens of identity avoidance, Salaita's detractors were able to demonstrate their presumed abhorrence of anti-Semitism—even as they highlighted ethnic difference as justification for his denunciation. At the same time, his identity was ignored as a potential source of spontaneous angry remarks given that the war in Gaza has created casualties among people of his cultural background.

Ironically, other tweets by Salaita also deemed controversial implicated Israel in fomenting anti-Semitism due to its ongoing war against Palestine. In other words, the tweets distinguished between anti-Semitism and antinationalism by drawing a distinction between Jewish people and the nation of Israel. In ignoring this vital difference, Palestinian and Jewish identity were erased under rubrics of nationalism. This rhetorical conflation renders Palestinians simultaneously hypervisible—as Western nations debate the legitimacy of Palestine or regard its citizens as radicals always at war with Israel—and invisible—since Western audiences overlook the casualties and material losses suffered by Palestinians as a result of the war against coloni-zation. Not so ironically, this un/seeing enables symbolic and physical violence against Jews as well by obscuring how fre-quently Jewish people themselves are framed as inferior or sus-pect citizens in the racial hierarchies that characterize Western society. Historically, Western societies have tended to regard Jews, like Muslims, as "foreign" and hypervisible, and their sup-posed threat to the social order has authorized their ghettoiza-tion and mistreatment (Kruger 1992, 301–23; Strickland 2003). These impressions persist, rendering Jewish people especially vulnerable to harm.

The easily shared nature of tweets means users can "gladly decontextualize the texts [they] share, or fragment them from their original contexts" so they appear to support novel inter-pretations (Johnson-Eilola 2008, 113). Under the guise of fighting anti-Semitism, many of Salaita's detractors pronounced racist judgements that reflected historical prejudices levied against both Muslims and Jews. And, in so doing, these judg-ments authorized the very same identity-avoidance frameworks that framed Salaita's hypervisibility not as a matter of ethnicism but of individual culpability. An analysis of the uproar corrobo-rates findings that digital media can make the erasure and exclu-sion of racialized bodies "pedestrian and nondiscriminatory" (Robinson 2015, 327). By playing on prejudices embedded in people's ways of knowing, a focus on specific aspects of Salaita's identity meant the larger issues related to the scandal—the war and the systemic racism and religious prejudice levied against both Palestinians and Jews—could be ignored.

Saida Grundy

The tendency for public attention to focus on select statements made by public intellectuals while disregarding the historical, intellectual, and structural origins of these comments informed a similar incident the following May. Saida Grundy, a Black soci-ologist newly hired by Boston University, became a target of conservative ire after some of her graduate school tweets were published on *Fox News*. The tweets, such as one that deemed college-aged white males a "problem population," were based on her research related to white masculinity on college campuses. Labeled by pundits and bloggers as "anti-white" and "a black racist," her detractors demanded that BU rescind the appointment. White student groups posted flyers on campus calling for her to be fired. Though Grundy did not lose her job, the university president officially denounced her comments, and she faced relentless online harassment.

As was the case with Salaita, identity avoidance allowed members of the public and fellow scholars to chastise Grundy for what they considered racist tweets. Political science professor Jason Johnson wrote, "This is not a matter of free speech or academic freedom, Dr. Gundy said some racist and likely factually incorrect things online. If a white female professor tweeted: 'If blacks in Baltimore would stop gang banging and having babies out of wedlock maybe they wouldn't riot' [p]eople would want her head and no African American student in their right mind would take her classes ever again even if she apologized" (2015). Although Johnson demonstrates concern that Grundy's online activities confirm every "wannabe conservative fanboy's" worst stereotype of the leftist liberal professor, his opinion piece interprets Grundy's tweet against the hypothetical tweet as though they bear equal weight.

By overlooking the importance of power differentials, Grundy is simultaneously framed as conspicuous to critics but also responsible for their increased surveillance of her online presence: her tweets incite and personify stereotypes—of the liberal professor, of the angry Black woman—rather than already being laden with those labels and forced into them retroactively. Those two stereotypes combine to make professional conditions challenging for Black women scholars, especially those who try to use their position in academia to enact social change within and outside the institution (Williams 2001, 89). On the one hand, institutions wishing to be perceived as active in working toward change are likely to hire scholars of color whose research reveals an activist bent; on the other, work by these scholars must

conform to whitestream ideals signified by discourses of professionalism, respectability, and collegial decorum.

The effects of identity segmentation and datafication make
this a precarious position for Black women scholars to inhabit.
Identity avoidance contributes to this catch-22 by insisting that
racism only exists as epithets or overt threats. All races now
being (ostensibly) equal, Grundy was framed as the sole party to
blame because she had isolated a specific demographic, white
males, and leveled accusations of wrongdoing at them based on
their racial identities. That her research relied on statistics or that
she was drawing attention to the carceral repercussions of structural racism did not matter. She had allegedly oppressed white
males in a public venue, despite a lack of agency to enact actual
oppression, and she had done so precisely because of her identity as a Black woman. These charges, like Johnson's analogy,
ignored how often Black people are accused of playing the race
card. Directly and allusively, they are typecast as troublemakers
who charge the dominant culture with racism as an excuse for
their own failings even and especially when they denounce the
everyday effects of racism.

Daniel Brewster

The following year, 2016, saw the online targeting of yet another
professor, this time due to his sexual orientation. The case
involved Milo Yiannopoulos's attack on Daniel Brewster, a sociology professor at West Virginia University. WVU's Republican
student group invited Yiannopoulos, the notorious conservative
pundit known for his flashy persona and his role as a writer for
Breitbart—an alt-right "news" site. Upon discovering Brewster
had planned an inclusive event that coincided with his speaking
engagement, Yiannopoulos attacked Brewster, calling Brewster
a "fat [homophobic slur]" and inciting his (Yiannopoulos's) followers to follow suit by pointing out that Brewster was on Twitter
(Beck, *Pittsburg Post-Gazette*, December 4, 2016). He mocked
Brewster's choice of discipline (communication studies) and
his participation in a multicultural LGBTQ event scheduled for

the same day as Yiannopoulos's appearance. He then accused
Brewster of being a bully who punished conservative students
who expressed their political views and derided Brewster's
Twitter profile, wherein he declared himself a student advocate,
as a source of contempt (Jaschik 2016).

Divorced from the political and ideological contexts in which
Brewster's tweets were posted, Brewster's profile established him
among his attackers as a social justice warrior all too ready to
take issue with those who were merely practicing their rights to
free speech. These rights included the ability to utter homophobic and fatphobic remarks and aim them at specific targets without repercussions. These appeals to free-speech rights hinged
on identity avoidance by framing all speech as equal—or equally
problematic—no matter who speaks and why. Brewster encouraged students to attend an inclusive event rather than attacking
Yiannopoulos or confronting him directly, but an open invitation to the event was framed as insult enough: the refusal to
listen to Brewster was an act of silencing under the semblance
of content-neutral "free speech." The selective interpretation of
his detractors focused on Brewster's actions while attempting to
erase their moral timbre and the need for such actions.

Furthermore, the identity avoidance that informed this situation seemingly legitimized Brewster's being harassed and
reinforced the homophobic social structures that endanger
LGBTQIA people, normalizing such harassment and increasing
the likelihood of its recurrence. These social structures create
problematic environments on college campuses, despite their
reputation as liberal spaces. Educational and social program-
ming are typically aimed at the cisgender, heterosexual whitestream, which can lead LGBTQIA students to self-isolate as they
seek out those they regard as their peers; and, because student
organizations are usually do not address intersectional needs
or identities, college life can prove especially difficult for students with multiply marginalized identities (Brown et al. 2004,
8–26: Poynter and Washington 2005, 41–47). At the cultural
level, Brewster's claim of harassment was cast by so-called free-
speech defenders as sham persecution concocted to sustain what

they perceived as homosexual "privilege." Proof of this idea lay in Yiannopoulos's own homosexual identity, which he used as an implicit justification for his attack on Brewster. In his typical shocking fashion, Yiannopoulos even used a homophobic slur in the title of his tour, calling it the *Dangerous [Slur] Tour*. Yiannopoulos and his fans adhered to a content-neutral impression of free speech that dislocated the slur and their fatphobic remarks from the history of oppression that has given these words significant cultural weight and from the harmful conditions they create. Appealing to the nation's collective right to freedom of speech, Yiannopoulos used his own identity to discount the power of homophobic language, even as he himself exploited this power and deployed it against Brewster and others.

In this situation, the paradox of identity avoidance, merged with attention to salient identity markers habituated by datafication's influence, foregrounded Brewster's and Yiannopoulos's homosexuality as if the men's identities were transposable. Yiannopoulos's public standing proved that because someone with his identity had been accepted by conservatives, discrimination against the LGBTQIA community was a thing of the past. It is especially ironic, then, that Yiannopoulos would be dismissed from his position at Breitbart after a video surfaced in which he defended pedophilia (Farhi, *Washington Post*, February 21, 2017). Stereotypes framing queer people, particularly gay men, as depraved or perverse are often used to attack LGBTQIA people and ruin lives. Using identity avoidance to secure his own social standing, Yiannopoulos affirmed injurious characterizations brought to bear on his own case. Despite losing his position at Breitbart, the harm he wreaked while there continues to harm many[5] (Ohlheiser, *Washington Press*, July 21, 2016).

DISCUSSION AND CONCLUSION

Incidents like those involving Salaita, Grundy, and Brewster illustrate how surveillance technologies naturalize the dominant perspective's authority to use identity markers to organize the physical and digital worlds. Coupled with identity-avoidant frameworks, surveillance can enable the online persecution of people speaking out against social inequalities that directly affect them. Salaita's harassment relied on ethnicism, Grundy's on racism and sexism, and Brewster's on homophobia, all in the name of decency. Identity avoidance was used to frame their cyber-harassment as based in moral indignation rather than a suppression of social justice concerns. These examples show that even those academics who do not consider themselves public figures must become more critically attuned to issues of public/private speech and surveillance.

While their cases received considerable media attention, Salaita, Grundy, and Brewster are not the only public intellectuals who have faced public backlash and persecution due to their social media activities. Nor are these cases singular in highlighting the use of social media to censure individuals perceived as having committed serious ideological infractions. Social media allow people to speak to publics beyond their immediate circles, amplifying their voices and allowing users to connect with others no matter where they are, whether for good or ill. Salaita and Grundy aimed to share insights gleaned from their research to reach those affected by the pressures they examined to effect social change, while Brewster's attackers used the medium to organize against him. This perceived "freedom" functions as a covert form of social management. As users participate in online rhetorical ventures, they take on the norms of designers, developers, and discourse communities that hone users' social, rhetorical, and epistemological expectations.

Dataveillance has real-world repercussions that contribute to the ideological climate of the times, from enabling racial profiling at airports and employment discrimination to influencing notions of health and bodily integrity (Haggerty and Ericson 2006; Mann, Nolan, and Wellman 2002, 331–55). On social media, users divide their identities into datasets, encouraging others to read them through and as dataset clusters and learning to read others accordingly. Dataveillance contributes to the use of identity-avoidant frameworks by highlighting seemingly neutral bits of data while obscuring the prejudices through which these datasets are chosen, assembled, and interpreted. Digital technology designs may seem arbitrary—or recede altogether due to maximum usability—but they are laden with issues of power and representation. Indeed, it is "when the technology disappears [that] ideologies are working the most strongly" (Beck 2013, 353). Critics have questioned how media representation affects popular impressions of identity, but one must ask also how everyday notions of identity are constructed through dataveillance and people's interactions with technology. Since media are the primary tools through which individuals are socialized into the hegemonic order (Littlefield 2008, 676), media also affirm identity avoidance by bolstering the ways through which users already un/see identity.

Combating harmful stereotypes on- and offline proves challenging because they are based in deeply and historically ingrained ways of selective knowing, and they continue to morph along with the changing social demographics. The segmentation characterizing social media datafication does not create or reconfigure these metrics but does make them more pronounced since users cannot present all aspects of their identities online. These technologies bolster identity-avoidant frameworks by advancing the idea that users have no choice but to draw on salient identity markers even if they choose not to do so ordinarily.

Scholars who are members of vulnerable groups are rendered hypervisible by social media logics that depend on systemic biases epistemologically. Academics who are targeted might lose their faculty positions or get censured by administrators for bringing undesirable attention to their home institutions (Bowman 2015, 357–58). In addition, the archival nature of social media (and digital media in general) generates an identity imprint that follows users. Words and personae remain available for public consumption, ready to be conjured by diverse audiences and laden with new significance. Posts and comments can be dislocated from their temporal, social, and political circumstances and advanced as authentic a priori proofs of a composer's intentions or beliefs. Despite these risks, social media use continues to prove popular, suggesting more research is necessary on how colonial and oppressive designs continue to inform the cultivation and interpretation of seemingly neutral digital data, as well as how these things affect scholarly endeavors. Datafication and dataveillance advance processes that enable social hierarchies in the physical world, and they encourage users to continue isolating and highlighting specific aspects of identity in cyberspace. Social regulation in the digital world must be understood as a vital aspect of real-world regulation and vice versa if users are to recognize how surveillance maintains order across the many spheres in which they live their lives.

NOTES

1. See chapter 2 in this collection, "Tinker, Teacher, Sharer, Spy: Negotiating Surveillance in Online Collaborative Writing Spaces," by Jenae Cohn, Norah Fahim, and John Peterson; and chapter 3, "Grades as a Technology of Surveillance: Normalization, Big Data, and the Teaching of Writing," by Gavin P. Johnson.

2. As is further evidenced in Santos Ramos's chapter (chapter 8).

3. *Dataveillance* can be defined as surveillance of one's electronic data, a process enabled by datafication, the translation of personal information into usable, representative bits of data.

4. Even critical race theorists often fall back on harmful impressions of disability despite a need shared with disability studies scholars to "(re)theorize difference as a historical, social, and economic construct . . . (re)constituted in complex ways by contesting ideological configurations" (Watts and Erevelles 2004, 276).

5. This no longer includes Twitter, as the platform banned Yiannopoulos for life following targeted racist attacks on actor Leslie Jones by Yiannopoulos and his followers.

REFERENCES

Amoore, Louise, and Marieke Goede. 2005. "Governance, Risk and Dataveillance in the War on Terror." *Crime, Law and Social Change* 43 (2): 151.

Angwin, Julia, and Hannes Grassegger. 2017. "Facebook's Secret Censorship Rules Protect White Men from Hate Speech but Not Black Children." *ProPublica*, June 28. https://www.propublica.org/article/facebook-hate-speech-censorship-internal-documents-algorithms.

Annamma, Subini A., Darrell D. Jackson, and Deb Morrison. 2017. "Conceptualizing Color-Evasiveness: Using Dis/ability Critical Race Theory to Expand a Color-Blind Racial Ideology in Education and Society." *Race Ethnicity and Education* 20 (2): 147–62.

Beck, Estee N. 2013. "Reflecting upon the past, Sitting with the Present, and Charting Our Future: Gail Hawisher and Cynthia Selfe Discussing the Community of Computers and Composition." *Computers and Composition* 30 (4): 349–57.

Beck, Estee N. 2015. "The Invisible Digital Identity: Assemblages in Digital Networks." *Computers and Composition* 35: 125–40.

Bowman, Timothy D. 2015. "Differences in Personal and Professional Tweets of Scholars." *Aslib Journal of Information Management* 67 (3): 356–71.

Brown, Robert D., Brandy Clarke, Valerie Gortmaker, and Rachael Robinson-Keilig. 2004. "Assessing the Campus Climate for Gay, Lesbian, Bisexual, and Transgender (GLBT) Students Using a Multiple Perspectives Approach." *Journal of College Student Development* 45 (1): 8–26.

Ceyhan, Ayse. 2012. "Surveillance as Biopower." In *Routledge Handbook of Surveillance Studies*, edited by Kirstie Ball, Kevin D. Haggerty, and David Lyon, 38–45. New York: Routledge.

Cross, Mary. 2011. *Bloggerati, Twitterati: How Blogs and Twitter Are Transforming Popular Culture*. Santa Barbara, CA: Praeger.

Friesen, Norm, Andrew Feenberg, and Grace Smith. 2009. "Phenomenology and Surveillance Studies: Returning to the Things Themselves." *Information Society* 25 (2): 84–90.

Gandy, Oscar H. 2012. "Matrix Multiplication and the Digital Divide." In *Race after the Internet*, edited by Lisa Nakamura and Peter Chow-White, 128–45. New York: Routledge.

Haggerty, Kevin D., and Richard V. Ericson, eds. 2006. *The New Politics of Surveillance and Visibility*. Toronto: University of Toronto Press.

Indiana University. 2013. "IU Receives Patent for Informatics Professor's Work Predicting Economic Activity through Twitter." IU News Room, February 19. http://newsinfo.iu.edu/news-archive/23831.html.

Jaschik, Scott. 2016. "West Virginia University Lets Controversial Speaker Appear and Answers His Attack on Professor." Inside Higher Ed, December 5. https://www.insidehighered.com/news/2016/12/05/west-virginia-university-lets-controversial-speaker-appear-and-answers-his-attack.

Jenkins, Richard. 2012. "Identity, Surveillance and Modernity: Sorting Out Who's Who." In *Routledge Handbook of Surveillance Studies*, edited by Kirstie Ball, Kevin D. Haggerty, and David Lyon, 159–66. New York: Routledge.

Johnson, Jason. 2015. "Opinion: Saida Grundy Shows Twitter Doesn't Always Equal Tenure." NBC News, May 16. http://www.nbcnews.com/news/nbcblk/oped-saida-grundy-twitter-doesnt-always-equal-tenure-n360026.

Johnson-Eilola, Johndan. 2008. "Communication Breakdown: The Postmodern Space of Google." In *Electronic Mediations: Small Tech: The Culture of Digital Tools*, edited by Byron Hawk, David M. Rieder, and Ollie Oviedo, 110–15. Minneapolis: University of Minnesota Press.

Kruger, Steven F. 1992. "The Bodies of Jews in the Late Middle Ages." In *The Idea of Medieval Literature: New Essays on Chaucer and Medieval Culture in Honor of*

Donald R. Howard, edited by Donald Roy Howard, Christian K. Zacher, and James M. Dean, 301–23. Newark: University of Delaware Press.

Levi, Michael, and David S. Wall. 2004. "Technologies, Security, and Privacy in the Post-9/11 European Information Society." *Journal of Law and Society* 31 (2): 194–220.

Littlefield, Marci B. 2008. "The Media as a System of Racialization: Exploring Images of African American Women and the New Racism." *American Behavioral Scientist* 51 (5): 675–85.

Lupton, Deborah, and Ben Williamson. 2017. "The Datafied Child: The Dataveillance of Children and Implications for their Rights." *New Media & Society* 19 (5): 780–94.

Lyon, David. 2001. *Surveillance Society: Monitoring Everyday Life*. Philadelphia: Open University Press.

Mann, Steve, Jason Nolan, and Barry Wellman. 2002. "Sousveillance: Inventing and Using Wearable Computing Devices for Data Collection in Surveillance Environments." *Surveillance & Society* 1 (3): 331–55.

Manovich, Lev. 2008. "Data Visualization as New Abstraction and as Anti-Sublime." In *Electronic Mediations: Small Tech: The Culture of Digital Tools*, edited by Byron Hawk, David M. Rieder, and Ollie Oviedo, 3–9. Minneapolis: University of Minnesota Press.

Mignolo, Walter. 2003. *The Darker Side of the Renaissance: Literacy, Territoriality, and Colonization*. Ann Arbor: University of Michigan Press.

Naber, Nadine. 2008. "Introduction: Arab Americans and U.S. Racial Formations." In *Race and Arab Americans before and after 9/11: From Invisible Citizens to Visible Subjects*, edited by Amaney Jamal and Nadine Christine Naber, 1–45. Syracuse, NY: Syracuse University Press.

Plummer, Joseph T. 1974. "The Concept and Application of Life Style Segmentation." *Journal of Marketing* 38 (1): 33–37.

Poynter, Kerry J., and Jamie Washington. 2005. "Multiple Identities: Creating Community on Campus for LGBT Students." *New Directions for Student Services* 111: 41–47.

Quijano, Aníbal. 2000. "Coloniality of Power, Eurocentrism, and Latin America." *Nepantla: Views from South* 1 (3): 533–80.

Robinson, Brandon A. 2015. "'Personal Preference' as the New Racism: Gay Desire and Racial Cleansing in Cyberspace." *Sociology of Race and Ethnicity* 1 (2): 183–215.

Sa'di, Ahmad H. "Colonialism and Surveillance." In *Routledge Handbook of Surveillance Studies*, edited by Kirstie Ball, Kevin D. Haggerty, and David Lyon, 151–158. New York: Routledge.

Said, Edward. 1979. *Orientalism*. New York: Vintage.

Salaita, Steven. 2006. *The Holy Land in Transit: Colonialism and the Quest for Canaan*. Syracuse, NY: Syracuse University Press.

Smith, Linda T. 2013. *Decolonizing Methodologies: Research and Indigenous Peoples*. New York: Zed Books.

Strickland, Debra H. 2003. *Saracens, Demons, and Jews: Making Monsters in Medieval Art*. Princeton: Princeton University Press.

Van Dijck, José. 2014. "Datafication, Dataism and Dataveillance: Big Data between Scientific Paradigm and Ideology." *Surveillance & Society* 12 (2): 197–208.

Veracini, Lorenzo. 2010. *Settler Colonialism: A Theoretical Overview.* New York: Palgrave Macmillan.

Villanueva, Victor. 2006. "Blind: Talking about the New Racism." *Writing Center Journal* 26 (1): 3–19.

Watts, Ivan E., and Nirmala Erevelles. 2004. "These Deadly Times: Reconceptualizing School Violence by Using Critical Race Theory and Disability Studies." *American Educational Research Journal* 41 (2): 271–99.

Williams, Charmaine C. 2001. "The Angry Black Woman Scholar." *NWSA Journal* 13 (2): 27–34.

8

CULTURAL POLITICAL ORGANIZING
Rewriting the Latinx "Criminal/Immigrant" Narrative of Surveillance

Santos F. Ramos

This chapter discusses the role surveillance plays in the framing of Latinxs as "immigrants" and "criminals" within popular discourse and how community organizers are rewriting this narrative by engaging in what I refer to as *cultural political organizing*. Rather than outright rejecting the labels of *immigrant* and *criminal*, cultural political organizing works to create visibility for the varied, complex positionalities of Latinxs, and it prioritizes establishing relationships both inside and outside an organization to build powerful community networks. I argue that in order to understand the full implications of this work, our analyses must make connections among the immigrant-detention system, the prison-industrial complex, and settler colonialism as the elements of an overarching framework that employs surveillance as a tactic aiming to bring about cultural and economic domination over Latinx and Indigenous communities. Within this context, I consider surveillance to be the literal tracking and identification of Latinx migrant communities by state entities such as the Department of Homeland Security. Additionally, I consider how, by extension, surveillance deploys narratives that disrupt the self-determination of diverse Latinx cultures.

By paying attention to the rhetorical composition strategies employed by community organizations, I highlight how Latinx community organizers are able to create pathways that help others build networks based on the concept of cultural political

DOI: 10.7330/9781646420315.c008

organizing, which simultaneously fights for the cultural self-determination of a given group and responds to the immediate threats imposed upon it via inequitable civil rights and other forms of discrimination. Therefore, in many ways this chapter is centered around detailing the positionality of Latinx as it is rhetorically constructed through various forms of media.

LITERATURE REVIEW

While approaches to surveillance studies are becoming increasingly varied, a common thread among most, if not all, scholars who relate their work to Latinx communities in particular is that surveillance is not simply a passive act of observation. Latinxs are surveilled for the explicit purpose of imposing violence upon their communities, perpetuating inequalities of who gets surveilled and how, whether through the direct threat of detention and deportation, or as I am also arguing, through the coercive pressures of assimilation. It is well documented among surveillance scholars that, since 9/11, the use of modern surveillance technologies has dramatically increased and that this increase has had a specifically important role in expanding immigrant-detention and -deportation systems in the United States and even in Mexico (Botello 2012, 2015; Pallito and Heyman 2008; Vélez 2012). Robert Pallito and Josiah Heyman, for example, consider how post-9/11 security programs like retinal scanning and vehicle preclearance employ unequal practices in regulating mobility into and within the United States (2008). Alejandro Vélez has analyzed the implications of a biometric ID card in Mexico that highlights how Mexicans "know and feel every day that they have more pressing needs that are being obviated by the government" (2012, 50). Other scholars have offered frameworks for doing surveillance studies specifically as it relates to Latin America, such as Nelson Arteaga Botello (2012, 2015), who has focused on building an agenda centered around analyzing violence and insecurity as central elements of surveillance in the region.

While it is clear that emergent technologies continue to shape how Latinx communities are being surveilled, scholars have expanded the definition of surveillance beyond a technology-driven focus. Scholars within the field have also centered their research around ways surveillance is created and produced within social interactions in everyday life (Newell, Gomez, Guajardo 2017; Green and Zurawski 2015). This research speaks to the importance of ethnographic methods within the field that could open up space for a wider array of experiences and knowledges related to surveillance to become more visible (Abu-Laban 2015). Furthermore, grounding research in the everyday experiences of the communities who are directly impacted by surveillance tactics does not exclude foci on the technologies themselves. In shifting our focus to how these technologies are being navigated by a particular population, space must also be made for interpreting the technologies from that community's cultural perspective.

As Adela C. Licona and Marta Maria Maldonado explain, Latinxs experience much tension around their own visibility as immigrants: "To be visible in community spaces means to be included . . . to have access to institutions and resources. By contrast, in the present context of entrenched anti-immigrant hostility and heightened immigration enforcement, for Latin@s . . . visibility . . . often entails standing out as an 'unbelonging' presence, being the subject of surveillance and policeability, of criminalizing, pathologizing, and otherwise alienating discourses and practices" (2015, 520). Licona and Maldonado also work to show how invisibility impacts Latinxs who have incarcerated and deported loved ones, rendering "an absence, an imprint, that is shaped by and shapes public rhetorics, social imaginaries and relations, dynamics, and politics for the family that is left behind, and for the community" (520). Using this framework, we can understand that surveillance pertains to the realm of visibility but also depends upon what Malea Powell describes as an "un-seeing" of the "foundation of blood and bodies upon which it constitutes itself" (1999, 10–11).

This unseeing plays out within discourse around immigration in the United States, typically failing to acknowledge the Indigeneity of many Latinxs by framing them simply as "immigrants." However, as Dylan Miner writes in an October 1, 2015, post to the *Decolonization: Indigeneity, Education, & Society* blog, "Immigration policy—in the USA, Canada, and even Mexico—cannot be understood outside a history of longer and deeper systemic and systematic appropriation of Indigenous lands and seizure of resources." So even though Latinxs in the southwestern United States are often referred to as "immigrants" and "illegals," Aja Y. Martinez explains that "we are neither newly arrived nor from Europe or other far-off countries . . . a large percentage of Chican@s, like me, have ancestral ties to the US Southwest and only became Americans when the border changed as a result of the Mexican-American War" (2016, 214–15).

And while it is essential to understand the physical and cultural violence enacted by the US-Mexico border, it is equally important to acknowledge, as Gabriela Raquel Ríos has, how settler nations continue to pillage the resources of peoples who are marked as Indigenous by the state (2016). I extend Rios's suggestion—that more writing studies scholars familiarize themselves with the framework of settler colonialism—to scholars of surveillance studies as well. Eve Tuck and K. Wayne Yang explain that "settler colonialism is different from other forms of colonialism in that settlers come with the intention of making a new home on the land, a homemaking that insists on settler sovereignty over all things in their new domain" (2012, 5). Therefore, even as Latinxs are often indigenous to the continent, it is essential to consider how the continuous process of displacement and immigration upholds the settler-colonial practices of the United States (and other nation-states) itself.

THE SETTLER SURVEILLANCE STATE

Despite the fact that some of the methods by which surveillance is carried out upon Latinxs have changed dramatically over the past few decades, the fundamental relationship between Indigenous people of the Americas and the settler surveillance state remains relatively unchanged. One of the ways

Spanish colonizers surveilled Indigenous communities was to
send out scribes to interview, observe, and compose descriptions of these "alien" cultures. This was a primary method
through which those in the "Old World" came to begin imag-
ining those Indigenous to the "New World" as savages and hea-
thens unworthy of humane treatment. Some mark February 23,
1521, as the first time a Spanish soldier appeared at the border
of P'urhépecha territory. Key to Spanish surveillance of the
P'urhépecha people for the purposes of conquest, as Afanador-
Pujol explains, "was gaining an understanding of P'urhépecha
political and territorial organization and history prior to the
first arrival of Europeans in 1521. Mendoza, who had come to
occupy the post of viceroy four years before his trip, probably
knew little about Michoacán. This may have been his reason for
commissioning a Spanish Franciscan friar at this time to record
the customs of the region. The 'Prologue' . . . states explicitly
that the friar created it at the viceroy's request to help him govern more efficiently" (2015, 2).

The surveillance set forth by Mendoza would later become
a published work known as the *Relación de Michoacán*, one of
the earliest surviving illustrated manuscripts from colonial
Mexico, and while many scholars have utilized the document as
a way of examining pre-Hispanic P'urhépecha society, perhaps
even attempting to preserve parts of the culture, its original
purpose was to prepare the Spanish for conquest (Afanador-
Pujol 2015). Through early colonial surveillance tactics such
as this, the Spanish Empire was better able to manipulate
Indigenous communities into submission, and it can be seen
that Western surveillance of Indigenous America has been carried out for the explicit purposes of political, cultural, and economic domination.

Underpinning the example above is a discursive interpretation
of surveillance that avoids conflation of digital surveillance technologies with surveillance itself. My line of analysis draws from the
work of Angela Hass, who in "Race, Rhetoric and Technology:
A Case Study of Decolonial Technical Communication Theory,
Methodology, and Pedagogy," maintains that rhetoric works to

upend prescribed and limited notions of race and technology and is therefore capable of both reinscribing traditional understandings of these terms and revising them in ways that lead to new understandings (2012). Highlighting people's tendency to conflate new media with definitions of technology, Haas shows that such rhetorical privileging of new over old obscures and erases diverse traditions of technological expertise; Haas argues, "It is critical that we interrogate the tension between technology as things, technology as work, and technology in relation to multiple and diverse actors when we grapple with the technicalities of technology" (2012, 289). In turn, I couch my understanding of surveillance within Haas's decolonial framework, which includes, yet is not exclusive to, the use of digital technologies of surveillance.

CREATING CRIMINALS

The work of Angela Davis in *Are Prisons Obsolete?* shows how criminals are fantasized as people of color in our collective imagination. "The prison," she argues, "therefore functions ideologically as an abstract site into which undesirables are deposited, relieving us of the responsibility of thinking about the real issues afflicting those communities from which prisoners are drawn in such disproportionate numbers" (2003, 16). As the US prison population has grown some 700 percent since 1970, Black, Native, and Latinx people have continued to be grossly overrepresented among that population, to the extent that criminal connotations have become attached to Indigenous people and people of color within the collective imagination of many US citizens (ACLU 2014, 2).

Many institutions are invested in the surveillance of migrant communities—from government agencies to private-prison companies, media conglomerates, vigilante groups, and more. A primary pillar among this network of organizations, however, is Immigration and Customs Enforcement (ICE). Created amidst the fear and paranoia of the 9/11 attacks, ICE became the single-largest government organization since the creation of the

Department of Defense and was granted a combination of civil and criminal authority through the Homeland Security Act of 2003. Under the Obama administration, ICE carried out more than 2.5 million deportations—more than any administration in US history. Even a casual glance at the rhetoric deployed by ICE through social media shows its great reliance on the concept of criminality in order to justify the existence and expansion of this profitable surveillance industry. The following headlines were taken from articles posted through ICE's Facebook page:

"Illegal Immigration is Not a Victimless Crime"

"ICE arrests alien wanted for homicide in Guatemala"

"HAVE YOU SEEN THIS MOST WANTED FUGITIVE? Convicted Aggravated Felon"

"South Texas ICE officers remove Salvadorian man wanted for aggravated homicide"

"ICE Arrests 400th Foreign Fugitive in Fiscal Year 2017" (ICE 2017)

The overwhelming majority of these headlines are in reference to Latinxs and often include pictures of Latinx people. If posts such as this are some people's primary window into Latinx communities, it is no wonder many seem to identify Latinxs in general as criminal aliens. This sweeping generalization was, of course, further validated by Donald Trump in his presidential campaign-launch speech when, in reference to Mexican immigrants, he openly stated, "They're bringing drugs. They're bringing crime. They're rapists."

Teresa A. Miller explains that today's provision of homeland security substantiates a vast, secretive, and racially driven security state that "increasingly . . . functions to socially control through confinement in secure disciplinary facilities the unpopular and the powerless, which in this case are undocumented people of color" (2002, 216).

There are currently roughly 209 detention facilities in the United States, with county- and state-run facilities also renting out additional beds to the federal government for the purposes of incarcerating undocumented migrants. The creation of

criminals is profitable for a number of private-prison companies, which have boasted record profit margins in recent years,
and the statistics show private prisons specializing in detained
undocumented immigrants is also an expanding venture.

Many of those detained and deported are dubbed *criminals*
strictly because of immigration-related offenses. The first deportation under the Trump administration was Guadalupe Garcia
de Rayos, a mother of two US-born citizens, whose "criminal"
status stems from a work-site raid nearly a decade before she was
deported in 2017. The "crime" she was responsible for, then,
was being an immigrant who migrated across a colonial border.
The situation in which immigrants are dubbed *criminals* simply
for being immigrants is not uncommon, and it highlights the
expanding overlap between criminal/immigrant categories for
Latinxs. While not totally new, the alarmist rhetoric employed
by the Trump administration, which perceives immigration as
a threat to the foundation of the United States itself, justifies
virtually any and all modes surveillance upon Latinxs in the
name of protecting the superiority of the country and ensuring
people's personal safety. This voyeuristic, settler-colonial perspective constitutes a form of rhetorical surveillance in which
Latinxs are watched and policed through commentary by various governmental agencies, politicians, and media.

SURVEILLING BACK, REWRITING
THE DOMINANT NARRATIVE

In her essay "Sounds of Surveillance: U.S. Spanish-Language
Radio Patrols La Migra," Dolores Inés Casillas explains the significant role Spanish-language radio has played in helping Latinx
communities navigate the complex immigrant-detention and
-deportation systems and even carry out surveillance techniques
against INS itself (2011). As one example, in response to a wave
of immigration raids, a community radio station (KDNA-FM)
in Yakima, Washington, assigned an individual to perform peri-
odic "INS watches" in the mornings. This "lookout" person
reported on suspicious-looking vehicles to inform listeners of

the possibility that INS was nearby. This "inverse-surveillance," as Casillas calls it, allowed immigrants to outwit the radar of the state and potentially avoid situations in which they could be indefinitely detained or deported from the country.

This example shows one way migrants have designed methods for evading detention and deportation and could be considered an example of what scholar Deanna Barenboim calls "spatial tactics of invisibility" (2016, 79). Barenboim argues that many aspects of the lives of migrants are filled with these kinds of tactics, and she writes also of how Maya migrants respond to the surveillance state by asserting their visibility as Indigenous people carrying out traditional cultural practices publicly. "A key site of tactical visibility," she claims, "is the cultural performance of jarana dance . . . an embodied form of expressive mobility [that] epitomizes cultural ideals of tranquilidad. Involving quick footwork, juxtaposed to poised stillness of the upper body, the dance form itself signals balance, evenness, and harmony" (2016, 87). Whereas tactics of invisibility, exemplified through the "INS watch" of a Spanish-language radio station, can help Latinxs resist a system that wishes to detain and deport them, spatial tactics of visibility call for the continuation of cultural practices (such as the jarana dance) in order to resist assimilation. Together, these two tactics help explain the dual identity many Latinxs have as both Indigenous people and migrants. Cultural political organizing, then, becomes essential, as it allows for flexibility in avoiding immigrant detention while also asserting cultural self-determination.

DAY OF THE DEAD ACTIONS

Latinx community organizers have long been drawing activism from the traditions of *El Día de los Muertos* (The Day of the Dead; referred to as Muertos from here on). Organizers within the Chicano movement of the 1960s and 1970s, for example, saw the holiday as an opportunity to connect their spiritual practices with struggles for social justice, often within the realms of education and immigration. Today, organizers continue to use traditions associated with Muertos for social justice causes, and this connection can especially be found in how they have carried out actions to honor and bring attention to those who have died while in immigrant detention. In this way, Latinxs are rewriting the criminal/immigrant narrative by drawing upon Muertos to root their political dissent in cultural tradition.

Octavio Pimentel explains that Muertos is "a designated time when family members and friends who have passed away are invited to join their living loved ones for a time of celebration" (2014, 260). While every region, pueblo, and even family may have its own set of traditions in accordance with Muertos, it is common for people to decorate sugar skulls, hold community processions, and build altars that commemorate the dead and/ or invite the dead back into their lives. Importantly, Cruz Medina writes that "while some argue that there is a lack of explicit connection between Día de Muertos and its Pre-Columbian roots, this argument remains indicative of the colonial project that sought to erase the history, literacy, and knowledge of Pre-Columbian populations through the burning of codices" (2016, 371). Exerting its pressure for Latinxs to remain invisible, the settler surveillance state attempts to erase Indigenous narratives and positions Latinxs exclusively as immigrants.

However, through cultural political organizing, organizers are working to counteract surveillance that seeks to integrate them into the mass incarceration system and flatten their ethnic identities. In 2016, a national coalition working to challenge the injustices of immigrant detention and deportation composed a call for nation-wide Day of the Dead actions spanning from October 26th to November 4th. The coalition created a document intended to educate communities about Muertos and offer pathways for building protest actions against the immigrant-detention system from cultural practices. The call exemplifies cultural political organizing because of its simultaneous emphasis on engaging in cultural continuance and on addressing immediate social justice issues impacting Latinx communities across the United States. This reliance on spiritual practice to address migrant social justice issues reflects the political and cultural complexity of Latinx positionalities within the United States at the same time it exemplifies how Latinx organizers have been able to rewrite the criminal/immigrant narrative by engaging in cultural political organizing that confronts and resists immigrant detention, deportation, and assimilation.

COMMUNITY DEFENSE ZONES

Community defense zones help create infrastructure for communities to respond efficiently and effectively to both the threat and the reality of deportation and detention. I would like to turn our attention now toward another document written by a separate grass-roots coalition operating within the immigrant-rights movement: the *Community Defense Zone Starter Guide*. As teachers and scholars, we stand to gain from observing the writing styles and rhetorical strategies of community organizers like the writers of this document, who are able to speak to complex policy issues and give analyses of power intended for a broad audience who may not have expertise in either of these arenas.

As exemplified in the starter guide, written communications attempt to create a pathway toward calculated action by moving readers through the following process: from context to goals, from goals to outreach.

Context

The establishment of relevant background information comes first in the *Community Defense Zone Starter Guide* (n.d.). This includes identifying the people and the organizations involved with creating the document, describing the political threat at hand, identifying the primary audience, and explaining how and why this guide can be used. In the following excerpt, a digestible political context is provided along with a clear solution that points toward the purpose of the document itself: "Across the country we see increased racism, injustice and criminalization just days into Trump's presidency. We know these problems didn't start with Trump—but we have real reason to believe these problems will escalate. Our silence will not stop what's happening" (1). In establishing the context for the community-defense guide, the document highlights the ways immigrants are criminalized on the level of community, and urgency is created around the need to come together and organize.

Goals

An overarching goal of the document is to highlight how "we might be able to reach beyond our existing circles, and engage non-activists we encounter in a variety of ways" (2). In this way, the primary "defense" of a community is the creation of community itself—an informed, networked, self-aware, and politically engaged community. The stated primary goals revolve around identifying "the needs of communities who are being attacked and targeted by long-standing and emerging policies and practices," getting local officials to support sanctuary for these communities, and recruiting a base of supporters and creating varying ways for community members to engage and support this work. In making its goals explicit, the document gives direction to the context described in its previous section and creates space for more specific tactics to be subsequently detailed.

Outreach

The "Outreach" section lays out a variety of pathways for achieving the stated goals, retaining the main purpose of building a base of human beings who support the campaign—that is, whatever specific project is being promoted or developed. The outreach described by the document involves a process of researching, meeting, evaluating, and following up with a variety of community entities. The suggested processes are tailored to the different kinds of community organizations referred to—doing outreach to local business as distinguished from doing outreach to student groups, civic-life leaders, and so forth. This section functions as a microcosm of the document itself, emulating the move from context to goals to action.

After describing the different outreach scenarios in detail, the document returns to some broader, more directional thinking: "We see the classic organizing outlined here as one kind of blueprint building us towards having local bases that leaders can mobilize towards action at needed times, and build with towards campaigns. We literally see a network of sign-ons as a base from which some people can be galvanized into a rapid response network" (23).

DISCUSSION

I have focused in this chapter on establishing as my exigence the interdependent relationship among immigrant detention and deportation, mass incarceration, and the settler-colonial surveillance state through looking closely at rhetorical composing strategies within Latinx communities. While the United States economy benefits in one sense from the unpaid/underpaid work of the undocumented migrant labor force, it is through this constellation of systems that surveillance is carried out upon Latinx communities in order to track, incarcerate, and deport large portions of the population. The pressure surveillance places upon these communities often forces them to assimilate out of their ethnic and cultural ways of identifying—in order to survive incarceration/deportation—and helps perpetuate narratives of Latinxs simply as immigrant or criminal.

Furthermore, surveillance of Latinxs (whether digital or not) is also a rhetorical struggle over identity; it shapes how Latinxs identify ethnically, as well as how Latinxs are identified by the state, the media, and other racial and ethnic groups. Through the identification of Latinxs as immigrants and criminals, surveillance of them becomes justified in the minds of many Americans. However, through the writing evidenced in the two calls to action I discuss, community organizations offer pathways toward organized resistance to surveillance while affirming the identities of Latinx people as migrants and/or Indigenous people. This two-pronged approach to community organization is what I describe with the term *cultural political organizing*.

It remains of utmost importance that scholars investigate how power dynamics of race and gender are inscribed in the digital technologies we use. As Christina Cedillo writes in this collection, "Digital technology designs may seem arbitrary—or recede altogether due to maximum usability—but they are laden with issues of power and representation" (145). Furthermore, not only is it necessary for scholars to recognize the relationship between power and technology, but they must also approach our understanding of these issues from the cultural perspectives of the communities we are working within. Doing so makes space for needed perspectives to emerge. In naming the historical example of colonial Spanish friars who were sent to document P'urhépecha culture as an early kind of surveillance technology, space was made to consider how surveillance uniquely impacts Indigenous people in contemporary society.

CONCLUSION

Tech companies such as Amazon, Palantir, Salesforce, and Microsoft are helping expand the capacity of US federal immigration agencies to detain and deport immigrants by providing ever-evolving technologies of surveillance. For this reason, it is critical for scholarship to interrogate the interplay of state and corporate power within the context of digital technologies, surveillance, and immigration rhetoric and to delineate how these technologies are being used to track and hunt down suspected undocumented people.

A growing number of social justice organizations are also working to make visible how the tech industry is profiting from the criminalization of Latinx communities. In a recent blog post, Mijente, a digital and grass-roots hub for Latinx and Chicanx community organizing, highlighted that the United States Marine Corps awarded a $13.5 million contract to Anduril Industries, Inc. to provide fully autonomous surveillance capabilities at four military bases, including one in Yuma, Arizona, near the US-Mexico border (2019). Organizers from the group explain that the "contract demonstrates the new frontier of surveillance, a surveillance apparatus where algorithms are trained to implement racist and xenophobic policies."

While the tech industry expands within the immigrant-detention system, and while organizers within the immigrant-rights movement counter new threats from both corporate and governmental entities, emerging digital forms of surveillance can be understood as an extension of centuries-old colonial surveillance. Latinx communities are putting cultural political organizing into action through their own forms of digital countersurveillance and through their writing practices, as well as through nontextual forms of communication and community building, in order to create broader narratives about who they are, where they come from, and the role they play in society. Exemplified by the writing of community organizations I discuss here, cultural and political elements are necessary in order for this organizing to be successful. Political organizing stripped of its cultural significance contributes to the forced assimilation of minority groups, and cultural organizing stripped of its contemporary political significance often fails to come to the aid of the most vulnerable members of a given community, such as those most at risk of being detained/deported.

REFERENCES

Abu-Laban, Yasmeen. 2015. "Gendering Surveillance Studies: The Empirical and Normative Promise of Feminist Methodology." *Surveillance & Society* 13 (1): 44–56.

Afanador-Pujol, Angélica J. 2015. *The Relación de Michoacán (1539–1541) and the Politics of Representation in Colonial Mexico.* Austin: University of Texas Press.

American Civil Liberties Union (ACLU). 2014. *Warehoused and Forgotten: Immigrations Trapped in Our Shadow Private Prison System.* ACLU. https://www .aclu.org/other/warehoused-and-forgotten-immigrants-trapped-our-shadow -private-prison-system.

Barenboim, Deanna. 2016. "The Specter of Surveillance: Navigating 'Illegality' and Indigeneity among Maya Migrants in the San Francisco Bay Area." *Political and Legal Anthropology Review* 39 (1): 79–94.

Botello, Nelson A. 2012. "Surveillance Studies: An Agenda for Latin America." *Surveillance & Society* 10 (1): 5–17.

Botello, Nelson A. 2015. "Doing Surveillance Studies in Latin America: The Insecurity Context." *Surveillance & Society* 13 (1): 78–90.

Casillas, Dolores. I. 2011. "Sounds of Surveillance: U.S. Spanish-Language Radio Patrols La Migra." *American Quarterly* 63 (3): 807–29.

Community Defense Zone Starter Guide. n.d. Georgia Latino Alliance for Human Rights, Mijente, Puente Movement. https://19lwtt3nwtm12axw5e31ay5s -wpengine.netdna-ssl.com/wp-content/uploads/2018/02/CDZ-Starter -Guide_ENG-021017.pdf.

Davis, Angela. 2003. *Are Prisons Obsolete?* New York: Seven Stories.

Green, Nicola, and Nils Zurawski. 2015. "Surveillance and Ethnography: Researching Surveillance as Everyday Life." *Surveillance & Society* 13 (1): 27–43.

Haas, Angela M. 2012. "Race, Rhetoric, and Technology: A Case Study of Decolonial Technical Communication Theory, Methodology, and Pedagogy." *Journal of Business and Technical Communication* 26 (3): 277–310.

Immigration and Customs Enforcement (ICE). 2017. "Immigration and Customs Enforcement (ICE)'s Facebook Page." Facebook. https://www .facebook.com/wwwICEgov.

Licona, Adela. C., and Marta M. Maldonado. 2014. "The Social Production of Latin@ Visibilities and Invisibilities: Geographies of Power in Small Town America." *Antipode* 46 (2): 517–36.

Martinez, Aja Y. 2016. "A Personal Reflection on Chican@ Language and Identity in the US-Mexico Borderlands: English-Language Hydra as Past and Present Imperialism." In *Why English? Confronting the Hydra*, edited by Pauline Bunce, Robert Phillipson, and Vaughan Rapatahana, 211–19. Bristol: Multilingual Matters.

Medina, Cruz. 2016. "Day of the Dead: Decolonial Expressions in Pop de los Muertos." In *The Routledge Companion to Latina/o Pop Culture*, edited by Frederick L. Aldama, 370–80. New York: Routledge.

Miller, Teresa. 2002. "The Impact of Mass Incarceration on Immigration Policy." In *Invisible Punishment: The Collateral Consequences of Mass Imprisonment*, edited by Meda Chesney-Lind and Marc Mauer, 214–38. New York: New Press.

Mijente. 2019. "Palantir Played Key Role in Arresting Families for Deportation, Document Shows." Mijente PAC. https://mijente.net/2019/05/palantir -arresting-families/.

Newell, Bryce C., Ricardo Gomez, and Verónica Guajardo. 2017. "Sensors, Cameras, and the New 'Normal' in Clandestine Migration: How Undocu- mented Migrants Experience Surveillance at the U.S.-Mexico Border." *Sur- veillance & Society* 15 (1): 21–41.

Pallito, Robert, and Josiah Heyman. 2008. "Theorizing Cross-Border Mobility: Surveillance, Security and Identity." *Surveillance & Society* 5 (3): 315–33.

Pimentel, Octavio. 2014. "El Día de Los Muertos." In *Encyclopedia of Latino Culture: From Calaveras to Quinceañera*, edited by Charles M. Tatum, 260–66. Santa Barbara, CA: ABC-CLIO-Greenwood.

Powell, Malea. 1999. "Blood and Scholarship: One Mixed-Blood's Story." *Race, Rhetoric and Composition*, edited by Keith Gilyard, 1–16. Portsmouth, NH: Boynton/Cook.

Ríos, Gabriela R. 2016. "Mestizaje." In *Decolonizing Rhetoric and Composition Studies: New Latinx Keywords for Theory and Pedagogy*, edited by Iris D. Ruiz and Raúl Sánchez, 109–24. New York: Palgrave Macmillan.

Tuck, Eve, and K. Wayne Yang. 2012. "Decolonization Is Not a Metaphor. Decolonization: Indigeneity." *Education & Society* 1 (1): 1–40.

Vélez, Alejandro. 2012. "Insecure Identities: The Approval of a Biometric ID Card in Mexico." *Surveillance & Society* 10 (1): 42–50.

Warren, J. Benedict. 1985. *The Conquest of Michoacán: The Spanish Domination of the Tarascan Kingdom in Western Mexico, 1521–1530.* Norman: University of Oklahoma Press.

Epilogue

WRITING IN A CULTURE OF SURVEILLANCE, DATAFICATION, AND DATAFICTIONS

Dànielle Nicole DeVoss

Technology is disappearing in terms of being naturalized. In a sense, technology disappears into the background. When the technology disappears, then ideologies are working the most strongly. (Cindy Selfe, in Beck 2013, 353)

We want to emphasize our role as rhetoric and writing scholars that privacy matters precisely because everyone remains entrenched in a data brokerage system that largely goes unchallenged or modified without active, collective resistance and protest. (Hutchinson and Beck, 8)

In the early-to-mid 1990s, in the position of a technology graduate assistant and through Michigan State University's writing center, I offered workshops on searching and evaluating the web. At that time, searching for relevant material on the web itself, using the premier search engine of the time, Yahoo, typically resulted in fewer than ten hits. Also, the current search engines (AltaVista and Lycos included) were case sensitive—so a search for "Madonna" and "madonna" resulted in different hits. Furthermore, cookies did not yet exist and browsers didn't maintain histories of our digital paths. Our phones weren't smart. Our software came packaged on CDs. Our data lived in notepads and on disks, not on networks and in clouds.

Integrated into these workshops was a discussion about how to understand and evaluate search-engine results. We often talked about why, when searching for, say, *telephone*, an ad for AT&T's phone services (at the time, of course, landline) appeared in the results. We also discussed emerging conversations fostered

DOI: 10.7330/9781646420315.c009

by the Federal Trade Commission (FTC) on guidelines related to whether and how search engines ought to be responsible for clearly identifying search-result content that was the results of paid placement or paid inclusion. In their chapter in this collection, Stephanie Vie and Jennifer Roth Miller draw from Casey Feisler, Cliff Lampe, and Amy Bruckman (2016) to suggest that policy—writ broadly and including end-user license agreements and terms-of-use expectations and law—"can be as powerful a design agent as technology. . . . However, its role is often considered only as an afterthought or when it becomes a problem" (chapter 6). Colleen Reilly's chapter, too, reminds us just how important such distinctions still are, but she also articulates that, because of how complex search-engine algorithms and technologies have become and how proprietary these systems are, it's more difficult to regulate—or to even see—what's happening under the digital surface of search results.

What's happening under the digital surface—and, indeed, across our screens, within our networks, and in our classrooms and streets and other surveilled physical spaces—is what this collection attends to. In 2020, the digital footprints of students, our colleagues, and ourselves are much broader and also much deeper than they were in the early 1990s. In this collection, Jenae Cohn, Norah Fahim, and John Peterson call attention to the spaces we use, and, specifically, the multiple, integrated, both diffuse and tight footprints (for instance, a user's Google profile can integrate across Google Docs, Google Maps, Google Search, and more, and across devices including smartphones, tablets, and computers). Dustin Edwards anchors our digital footprints to the spaces our bodies literally inhabit and the ways hypercirculation and hypersurveillance happen—in his case, via his Fitbit in a YMCA. This networked technology takes his heartbeat and other personal, embodied data via an app called Mywellness beyond the confines of his neighborhood Y, his neighborhood, his state, and the United States to the Mywellness company headquarters in Italy, and thus through European Union and Italian law. Jason Tham and Ann Hill Duin consider the institutional adoption of Fitbit technology at Oral Roberts University in the context of academic data collection, institutional priorities, and questionable surveillances. They argue that "in the face of pervasive computing and data mining, however, a critical awareness of digital literacy that focuses on the cultural, political, and other social aspects of technology must be supplemented by a contextual consideration of agency" (chapter 5). Indeed, we must ask about the why, who, what, and where of data-collection practices as they impose themselves on our bodies, in our classrooms, and across our devices.

It's tempting to anchor our discussion of technology and surveillance to more contemporary practices, but Santos Ramos, in chapter 8, reminds us of the long-held and long-deployed colonial strategies of surveillance, taking us back to the Spanish Empire and historical means of controlling individuals and communities. Christina V. Cedillo argues that "surveillance, dataveillance, and data segmentation—and their uses in social regulation—are not new but entrenched technologies now deployed in the digital realm. It is necessary to stress this point because these processes have long been exploited by dominant groups to regulate entire populations and assert power vis-à-vis epistemic authority" (chapter 7). There is much we can learn from the ways we might see surveillance as long-tailed, long-term strategy and not necessarily something "new" or emergent in the context of digital technologies. There is also much we can learn from the ways different individuals and communities have subverted surveillance practices; in this collection, this includes community activists who use Spanish-speaking radio to report on the presence of INS officials in Yakima, Washington (Ramos, drawing on Casillas [2011]).

One of the themes that emerges in this collection is that *we participate* in current digital surveillance contexts. In the introduction, the editors suggest that "we all, in some fashion, participate in the surveillance state that has been designed for our social and professional 'betterment.'" Cohn, Fahim, and Peterson, in describing their work with Google Docs in their classrooms, note that "we make this choice while engaging

with the risks of this choice" (chapter 2). Each chapter wrestles
with our complicity in creating data trails; participating in or
allowing digital surveillances; and engaging systems that are, in
part, designed to circumvent privacy. Gavin P. Johnson compellingly invites us to question our participation in these systems.
He's speaking specifically of systems of assessing, documenting,
and fixing grades, but his warning applies far beyond grading
machines; grades are just one example of "an imperfect system
of communication and corrupt technology of surveillance that
serves a neoliberal university that values control, individualism,
and financial gains above the critical, creative, and rhetorical
education of its students" (chapter 3). Indeed, we could readily
replace "university" with many other spaces (including, importantly, nonprofits; Colleen Reilly notes the surveillance bots run-
ning under the national Habitat for Humanity web site), and
"students" with a range of other terms—citizens, workers, family
members, community activists, to name just a few.

   Another theme that emerges is that how privacy impacts
identity. In this collection, Cohn, Fahim, and Peterson report
that "divorcing identity from written work allowed greater
freedom and flexibility" for students working in Google Docs,
where "coveillance . . . builds accountability and knowledge
construction" (chapter 2). The *when* and *how* of surveillance
is, of course, critical context, as is the *when* and *how* of identity. Cedillo reports on the ways identity avoidance within the
context of social media reinscribes ways of seeing, understanding, and being. She also calls attention to the fact that not only
are we generating identity imprints that follow us across media
and spaces, but all of us must "become more critically attuned
to issues of public/private speech and surveillance" (chapter
7). This is an uncomfortable space for many of us to dwell in,
especially in the context of "academic freedom" and a sense
that one's classroom door creates an intimacy and ensures a
private-ness.

   What this collection so powerfully and persuasively demonstrates is that computers and writing researchers are attending to widespread surveillance and advocating for privacy

protections from a unique perspective—one that attends to literacy practices, public writing, and the social construction of knowledge. One that attends to cultural dynamics and rhetorical attentions in an intersectional way. One that contributes to an ongoing conversation oriented toward not just rejecting but *negating* the notion that any tool, any technology, or any approach can be neutral. Indeed, as the editors and as the chapter authors articulate, all tools, all technologies, and all approaches carry with them the marks of designers, developers, coders, advertisers, and the many others who circulate around or directly participate in the production of these things. Reilly persuasively draws upon Estee Beck (2015) in this collection to argue that "users in digital environments interact constantly with virtual objects whose agency requires understanding and interrogation" (chapter 1). The editors here push past "singular, universal views" or "protectionist" versus "conservative" ideologies, and the authors offer critical, constellated orientations, including that technologies are not neutral but bring with them traces (sometimes overt, sometimes transparent) of power, preferences, realities, and so forth.

The collection attends to pedagogy and to the ways rhetoric and composition studies, and specifically computers and writing scholars, can equip students (and ourselves and our colleagues) to navigate the datafications and datafictions surrounding us and to think more deeply and more critically about unimagined and unknown and unanticipated audiences related to surveillance and "outside actors" like those mentioned by Cohn, Fahim, and Peterson. We are, indeed, composing with our clicks, our downloads, our purchases, and our searches.

The editors compellingly argue that our institutions are too readily offering data to external companies, private contractors, and software developers. Indeed, this collection in its entirety directly offers or at least points toward ways we can help our institutional administration, of course including our information and instructional technology units, to better understand the rewards and consequences of sharing faculty and student data.

Although the technologies discussed in this collection will likely come and go, evolve and be replaced (including Mozilla's Lightbeam, Cliqz's Ghostery, etc.), the concerns surfaced in this collection will likely not. The chapters here illuminate our need to continue to attend to related questions and issues, and to do so in a way that looks back and contextualizes the present historically but also looks toward and attends to future possibilities. In the spirit of the editors' introduction, and their move to situating the collection as a beginning to many necessary conversations about surveillance, I want to conclude first by centering two compelling questions Tham and Hill Duin pose in their chapter:

- How might writing scholars and instructors participate in the shaping of future programs and related policies on academic data collection?
- How might we best make transparent to instructors and students the many contexts within which data is collected and used? How might we problematize data ownership and work to build informed data generators? (chapter 5)

And I also want to add to these two questions a list of questions I both hesitantly and excitedly leave this collection with:

- How can we engage and enact Dustin Edwards's notion of "deep circulation," attentive to "cultures, communities, environments, and bodies" through "affective . . . textual . . . and infrastructural" flow? (chapter 4).
- As the editors ask in their introduction, what might contributions to our conversations about surveillance look like that hone in specifically on its effects on ability, gender, and sexual identity?
- How do we address the fact that certain conditions of surveillance affect different bodies and different digital presences differently?
- How do we wrestle with certain conditions of surveillance affecting individuals differently than they do communities?
- What questions must we ask and protections must we demand as more and more apps pose the potential of deeply and concurrently mapping both our physical and digital daily lives (geographically, economically, communicatively, and more)?

- What would ethical, participatory institutional approaches to data collection and analysis look like? What models exist that we can draw from now? What models can we innovate?

- How do we continue to engage work that that builds from both Tim Berners-Lee's and the editors' "sense of collaboration, education, and empowerment?" How can we, more specifically, model and share nimble, flexible practices directed toward ethical, appropriate, and critical ways of gathering and using data?

- Given that many of our students will go on to work within large (and small) organizations and companies gathering data, and/or will be expected to work with, analyze, and use user data, how can we best equip students to be ethical *readers and users* of data? To be ethical coders, programmers, and designers of data-collection measures?

- What will happen when the tools and infrastructures we've used to productively, ethically, humanely collect data to forward our work (e.g., humane data-driven assessment measures created within a writing program) break down? Become obsolete? Have we built in a way we can migrate that data? Or have we built in a way that data will disappear?

- How might more open-sharing and open-source accessibility to data change our conversations?

- How can we engage in "deep circulation" in ways that enable and equip us to also engage in "deep citizenship" (Edwards, this collection)?

- How can we better map, constellate, and understand the multiple networks under our current devices, where the internet is no longer a simple (if it ever was, in any way, simple) conduit to information but where information sails across spaces supported by the internet (e.g., the web) but also spaces created across various wireless and other connectivities?

- How do we navigate the complex relationship we have within networks of surveillance, privacy, and our desire to connect across social media spaces? How do we mediate being surveilled when being online is a necessary facet of our lives?

Overall, the collection forces us to wrestle with a reality many of us feel comfortable overlooking or bypassing on an everyday basis: the ways we exist in, and also willingly participate in, a context of digital surveillance. As Tham and Hill Duin implore in their chapter, users should "rethink what they consider to be private and public and recognize the rhetorical contexts wherein their privacy and identities must be negotiated" (chapter 5). As rhetoricians and as teachers of writing, we are well equipped to do this rethinking and engage this recognizing—and not only to rethink and recognize but to act, to advocate, and to assert. This collection provides us with the tools, the means, the rationale, and the rhetorical agency to do so.

REFERENCES

Beck, Estee N. 2013. "Reflecting upon the past, Sitting with the Present, and Charting Our Future: Gail Hawisher and Cynthia Selfe Discussing the Community of Computers and Composition." *Computers and Composition* 30 (4): 349–57.

Beck, Estee N. 2015. "The Invisible Digital Identity: Assemblages in Digital Networks." *Computers and Composition* 35: 125–140.

Casillas, Dolores Inés. 2011. "Sounds of Surveillance: U.S. Spanish-Language Radio Patrols La Migra." *American Quarterly* 63 (3): 807–29.

Feisler, Casey, Cliff Lampe, and Amy S. Bruckman. 2016. "Reality and Perception of Copyright Terms of Service for Online Content Creation." In *Proceedings of the 16th Conference on Computer-Supported Cooperative Work and Social Computing*, 1–12. New York: Association for Computing Machinery.

ABOUT THE AUTHORS

Estee Beck works as an assistant professor of technical and professional writing/digital humanities in the Department of English at The University of Texas at Arlington.

Christina V. Cedillo is an assistant professor of writing and rhetoric at the University of Houston–Clear Lake. Her research draws from cultural rhetorics and decolonial theory to focus on embodied rhetorics and rhetorics of embodiment at the intersections of race, gender, and disability. Her work has appeared in *Feminist Studies in Religion, Argumentation and Advocacy, Present Tense, Composition Forum*, and various edited collections. Her current project examines the multimodal rhetorics of twentieth and twenty-first-century women of color activists. She is the lead editor of the *Journal of Multimodal Rhetorics*.

Jenae Cohn is an academic technology specialist in the program in writing and rhetoric at Stanford University, where she supports students and instructors in incorporating critical digital pedagogy into the teaching of writing. She has published in *Computers and Composition, Transformative Dialogues, Kairos*, and edited collections about ePortfolio pedagogy and social annotation.

Dànielle Nicole DeVoss is professor, associate chair, and director of graduate studies for the rhetoric and writing program in the Department of Writing, Rhetoric, and American Cultures at Michigan State University. Her research interests include computer/technological literacies, digital-visual rhetorics, social and cultural entrepreneurship, innovation and creativity, and intellectual property issues in digital space. DeVoss coedited (with Heidi McKee and Dickie Selfe) *Technological Ecologies and Sustainability*, the first title to be published by Computers and Composition Digital Press, the first digital press in the United States with a university press imprint. The book is available at: http://ccdigitalpress.org/tes/. DeVoss has most recently published *Making Space: Writing Instruction, Infrastructure, and Multiliteracies* (with Jim Purdy; 2016, University of Michigan Press/Sweetland Digital Rhetoric Collaborative); *Type Matters: The Rhetoricity of Letterforms* (with C. S. Wyatt; 2017, Parlor Press); and *Explanation Points: Publishing in Rhetoric and Composition* (with John Gallagher; 2019, Utah State University Press).

Dustin Edwards is an assistant professor and the director of graduate programs in the Department of Writing and Rhetoric at the University of Central Florida. Attending to the environmental effects of big data, his current research works at the intersections of digital, environmental, and material rhetorics. His work has been or will soon be published in journals such as *Computers and Composition, Computers and Composition Online, Enculturation, Present Tense*, and *Rhetoric Review*, as well as in edited collections such as *Circulation, Writing, and Rhetoric* and *Digital*

Ethics: Rhetoric and Responsibility in Online Aggression. His email is dustin.edwards @ucf.edu.

Norah Fahim teaches in the program in writing and rhetoric (PWR) at Stanford University and holds the position of associate director at the Hume Center for Writing and Speaking. Prior to teaching at PWR, Norah taught in the University of Washington's expository writing program (EWP), where she received her PhD in language and rhetoric and a master's degree in TESOL (teaching English to speakers of other languages). Norah's research areas include narrative inquiry, writing program administration, TESOL, and second-language writing. Through narrative inquiry, her research focuses on the experiences of students utilizing digital platforms for composition. Her research also focuses on non-TESOL trained TAs working with an increasingly multilingual student population, as well as the experiences and needs of multilingual students, to better help advocate for the needs of multilingual learners within the classroom, the writing center, and at a wider institutional level.

Ann Hill Duin is a professor of technical communication at the University of Minnesota, where her research and teaching focus on digital literacy, analytics, and radical collaboration.

Les Hutchinson Campos is, as of 2021, an assistant professor of English at Boise State University. There, they teach courses on grant writing, social media content strategy, and decolonial approaches to technical documentation through service-learning partnerships with nonprofit organizations in the Boise area. Les conducts research at the intersection of cultural and digital rhetorics, as well as technical communication. As a queer, disabled Chicanx person with Indigenous descendency, they strive to do work in the world that is accessible, responsible, and relational with her communities and the land in the long-term project of decolonization.

Gavin P. Johnson (he/him) works as an assistant professor in the Department of Literature and Languages at Christian Brothers University in Memphis, Tennessee. There he and students collaboratively delink assessment and learning practices from dangerous racist, sexist, classist, ablest, and cisheteronormative traditions. He specializes in multimodal composition, cultural rhetorics, queer theory, and digital activism. His scholarship is published or forthcoming in *College Literacy and Learning, Composition Studies, Computers and Composition, Constellations: A Cultural Rhetorics Publishing Space, Peitho: The Journal of the Coalition of Feminist Scholars in the History of Rhetoric and Composition, Pre/Text: A Journal of Rhetorical Theory, Teacher-Scholar-Activist,* and various edited collections. He is a proud first-generation college graduate from southeast Louisiana.

John Peterson is an advanced lecturer in the program in writing and rhetoric at Stanford University. His current project is a book-length inquiry into improvisation as a learned activity involving practice and imagination: *Improvisation and Free Speech: The Danger and Beauty of Speaking Off-the-Cuff.*

Santos F. Ramos is an assistant professor of integrative, religious, and intercultural studies at Grand Valley State University. He holds a PhD in rhetoric and writing from Michigan State University, with a specialization in cultural rhetorics. In his work, he uses food, music, and cultural education to address issues related to immigration, Indigenous food sovereignty, and technology.

Colleen A. Reilly is professor of English and faculty associate for the Centers for Teaching Excellence and Faculty Leadership at the University of North Carolina Wilmington. She teaches undergraduate courses in professional and technical writing, including Introduction to Professional Writing, Document Design, Writing about Science, Digital Composing, and Writing and Activism, and graduate courses in science writing, research methods, and genders, sexualities, and technologies. She has published articles and book chapters related to search-engine optimization (SEO) and technical communication pedagogies, science communication pedagogies, gender and bioenhancement, privacy and surveillance in digital spaces, and entrepreneurship in technical communication programs.

Jennifer Roth Miller is a faculty member at the University of Central Florida in the Nicholson School of Communication and Media. Jennifer's work seeks to better understand digital citizenship and social media engagement by exploring the convergence of communication, technology, philanthropy, and education in socially constructing collective views and actions for social justice. Jennifer's work has been published in journals such as *Xchanges* and *Enculturation: A Journal of Writing, Rhetoric, and Culture*. She is also a coauthor of two book chapters in edited collections, one published by Routledge and the other published by University Press of Colorado.

Jason Tham (he/they) is an assistant professor of technical communication and rhetoric at Texas Tech University. He studies and teaches design thinking, user experience research, information design, and radical collaboration.

Stephanie Vie is professor of English and associate dean of the Outreach College at the University of Hawai'i at Mānoa. She researches digital technologies and their relationship with privacy and surveillance, most notably social media and video games. Her work has appeared in journals like *First Monday, Computers and Composition, Technical Communication Quarterly*, and *Computers and Composition Online*, and she is the editor or coeditor of the books *Social Writing/Social Media* and *e-Dentity*.

INDEX